MISERY AND ITS CAUSES

AMERICAN SOCIAL PROGRESS SERIES
EDITED BY
SAMUEL McCUNE LINDSAY, PH.D., LL.D.
COLUMBIA UNIVERSITY

A series of handbooks for the student and general reader, giving the results of the newer social thought and of recent scientific investigations of the facts of American social life and institutions. Each volume about 200 pages.

1. **THE NEW BASIS OF CIVILIZATION.** By SIMON N. PATTEN, PH.D., LL.D., University of Pennsylvania. Price $1.00 net.

2. **STANDARDS OF PUBLIC MORALITY.** By ARTHUR TWINING HADLEY, PH.D., LL.D., President of Yale University. Price $1.00 net.

3. **MISERY AND ITS CAUSES.** By EDWARD T. DEVINE, PH.D., LL.D., Columbia University. Price $1.25 net.

4. **GOVERNMENTAL ACTION FOR SOCIAL WELFARE.** By JEREMIAH W. JENKS, PH.D., LL.D., Cornell University. Price $1.00 net.

5. **SOCIAL INSURANCE.** A Program of Social Reform. By HENRY ROGERS SEAGER, PH.D., Columbia University. Price $1.00 net.

6. **THE SOCIAL BASIS OF RELIGION.** By SIMON N. PATTEN, PH.D., LL.D., University of Pennsylvania.

7. **SOCIAL REFORM AND THE CONSTITUTION.** By FRANK J. GOODNOW, LL.D., Columbia University. Price $1.00 net.

8. **THE CHURCH AND SOCIETY.** By R. FULTON CUTTING, LL.D.

THE MACMILLAN COMPANY
64–66 Fifth Avenue, New York

AMERICAN SOCIAL PROGRESS SERIES

MISERY
AND ITS CAUSES

BY

EDWARD T. DEVINE, Ph.D., LL.D.

SCHIFF PROFESSOR OF SOCIAL ECONOMY, COLUMBIA UNIVERSITY, GENERAL SECRETARY OF THE CHARITY ORGANIZATION SOCIETY OF THE CITY OF NEW YORK, AND EDITOR OF "THE SURVEY"

New York
THE MACMILLAN COMPANY
1912

All rights reserved

COPYRIGHT, 1909,
BY THE MACMILLAN COMPANY.

Set up and electrotyped. Published May, 1909. Reprinted
January, 1910; March, July, December, 1911; August, 1912.

Norwood Press
J. S. Cushing Co. — Berwick & Smith Co.
Norwood, Mass., U.S.A.

PREFACE OF THE EDITOR

Professor Devine's "Misery and its Causes," like Professor Patten's "New Basis of Civilization," with which this series began, attempts to articulate a new social philosophy, pragmatic, economic, and socially adaptable to the existing conditions of American life. Both volumes contain in substance the Kennedy lectures for the year of their respective publication, as prepared for the School of Philanthropy on a foundation made possible through the generosity of Mr. John S. Kennedy, for the express purpose of creating a literature of social work which shall guide, inspire, and make more efficient the busy practical worker who must replenish from time to time the sources of his energies in order to serve with power.

With fascinating realism, with astonishing concentration, with the keenest insight and interpretation of the results of an unusually rich, deep, and varied personal experience, and with a charm of style and a perfectly irresistible optimism in treating some of the saddest facts of human life, Professor Devine has placed

PREFACE OF THE EDITOR

us all under lasting obligations not only for a better understanding of the causes of misery, but also for the realization of the fact that there is a prophylaxis of misery and the promise of a real world in which it will be reduced by social control to manageable proportions.

SAMUEL McCUNE LINDSAY.

NEW YORK CITY,
April 20, 1909.

PREFACE

For a little over a dozen years it has been my duty and my opportunity to know something of the misery of the poor in New York. I am quite aware that there are many to whom that span of experience will seem brief and inconclusive. Let me avert this objection by a disclaimer against the inference that I am relying for my conclusions entirely upon my own personal experience and observation.

First of all I have had the benefit of the daily experiences of my associates in the General Work of the Charity Organization Society; of my associates in the publication offices of *Charities and the Commons*,[1] who are gathering in assiduously, week by week, a worldwide experience in social work; of my associates in the School of Philanthropy, directors, instructors, research fellows, and students; and of my colleague, the director of the Department for the Improvement of Social Conditions, and his staff.

This survey of modern misery has thus a somewhat

[1] This journal has been rechristened *The Survey* while this volume is in press.

PREFACE

broader basis than any one personal experience with dependent families, illuminating and instructive as that case work alone would be if it could be fully analyzed and interpreted. It so happens, further, that within the past two years I have had some personal connection with three special inquiries, each of which reveals certain aspects of the lives of workingmen which do not necessarily and regularly enter into the experiences of the charitable societies and which are yet to be considered in any study of modern misery. I refer to the Pittsburg Survey, carried out by the Charities Publication Committee, to the investigation of the Standard of Living, under the auspices of the State Conference of Charities and Correction, and to an investigation of the need for an employment bureau in New York City.[1] There have been numerous other inquiries which throw light upon our subject, but I refer to these three because it happens to have been my duty to be intimately in touch with them and to know their results. I shall not attempt to present their results in these lectures, but it is only reasonable to point out that such views as I set forth as to the character and causes of the misery which we encounter in the tenements of New York and other modern com-

[1] These three investigations were made possible by appropriations by the Russell Sage Foundation.

PREFACE

munities have been hammered out on the anvil indeed of my own observation and such capacity as I have for getting the general bearing of things, but by the sledge-hammer blows of facts recorded by agents and visitors as a result of their daily visits, and of investigations made under different auspices and by wholly different methods which have no other purpose in view except to disclose facts as they are.

For valuable suggestions in all parts of this study, for the analysis of the five thousand family records on which much of it is based, for the preparation of the diagrams, and for revision of proof sheets, I am under deep obligations to my assistant, Miss Lilian Brandt.

E. T. D.

NEW YORK,
March, 1909.

CONTENTS

CHAPTER		PAGE
I.	POVERTY AND MALADJUSTMENT	1
II.	OUT OF HEALTH	51
III.	OUT OF WORK	113
IV.	OUT OF FRIENDS	147
V.	THE ADVERSE CONDITIONS IN DEPENDENT FAMILIES	165
VI.	THE JUSTICE AND PROSPERITY OF THE FUTURE	237

CHAPTER I

POVERTY AND MALADJUSTMENT

I

LIKE the blind old Puritan of whose birth we have but lately celebrated the three hundredth anniversary, I seek the causes of human misery. Milton's theme is my theme — though you may think his theological and mine sociological. He with poetic license, with spiritual vision, with an assumption of dogmatic authority, and withal with revolutionary audacity, examined the phenomena that brought death into the world and all our woe. I am attempting, without dogma, without the warrant of other inspiration than that which guides the humblest disciple of science, and with no poetic invention, to examine with you the circumstances which bring premature, unnatural — what Metchnikoff calls violent — death among the children of men; and the causes of that misery which, whatever its origin, though it may indeed be the fruit of man's first disobedience, prompted by the guile of the infernal serpent, is nevertheless being perpetuated by the present voluntary actions of men, and so is a proper subject for our frank and earnest deliberation.

MISERY AND ITS CAUSES

If this were not so, if misery were inevitable, then there would be no justification for the new view of charity. If it is justified, it carries us irresistibly beyond the remedial agencies, beautiful and healing though they may be, to the consideration of the causes which bring them their tasks.

Although misery is our theme rather than poverty, or dependence, or pauperism, yet it is obvious that there are causes of misery that lie beyond the boundaries of this inquiry. Remorse over some past misconduct, the total failure of some high ambition, disappointment in love, the loneliness which comes from the inability to make friends, the silent anguish of a parent's broken heart, and a vast number of other such experiences which are familiar enough, do not readily lend themselves to social investigation or to conscious remedial social endeavor. There is, however, no sharp line between such mental anguish as lies in these experiences and that which is directly traceable to preventable disease and accident, to loss of employment and a low standard of living, to intemperance and vice and crime, to ignorance and inefficiency, and to the other well-recognized causes of dependence and misery among the poor.

We are to consider, then, not all misery, but such misery as gives external, objective indication of its

POVERTY AND MALADJUSTMENT

existence and its extent and its character. We shall seek not the ultimate explanation of misery which shall correlate the unhappy millionaire with the penniless outcast, and measure on the same scale their merit and their rewards, their shortcomings and their punishments; but rather such obvious and, if you please, more superficial explanations as will enable us to understand the surplus misery of those whose hardships bring them demonstrably to public attention.

II

The pictures of misery made familiar to us by Milton and Dante, and by many a sermon and novel, have this in common — that the misery of which they speak is punishment. It is the result of depravity, of the deliberate choice of evil. It is eternal, not to be ended, not to be mitigated, and still not to be borne. It is without hope, though the human mind refuses to compass the thought of the soul without hope. The misery of the infernal regions, especially as it is depicted by the Italian poet, is the logical working out of qualities of human character. There is an appropriateness, a poetic justice, about each of the various states of the fallen spirits, because they are but the projection of desires which have been indulged, of tendencies which have been encouraged, of appetites which have been fed, of passions to which control has been given over the lives of men.

This is one view also of the misery which we find here on earth, in prisons and hospitals, in homes and highways, in the haunts of vice and the hidden places of sorrow and shame. There is comfort for those who are not miserable in the theory that misery is but the natural working out of human character, that it is due to natural depravity, to deliberate wrong-doing and a conscious choice of evil ways, in the theory that suffering is proof of sin; and because of this satisfaction this view becomes the conventional, orthodox view. The sufferings of the tormented in hell by sound theology are imputed to wickedness on earth. It is an easy transition to impute the sufferings of the poor on earth to the same cause. Here, however, theology fails us, and the orthodoxy which insists upon this explanation is not of the religious kind, though it may seat itself in the church pew. It is rather the orthodoxy of a certain social philosophy against which every great religious teacher lifts his voice in indignant protest, against which every scientific observer records his testimony.

The assumption that misery is moral rather than economic; that those who are in distress for the lack of necessities of life are to be considered, without further evidence, as needing discipline even though they may need relief also, does not, it is true, rest exclusively upon the feeling of personal superiority to which I have attributed it. It is a stern doctrine thoroughly interwoven into a vast quantity of literature and into almost the whole of our charitable tradition.

MISERY AND ITS CAUSES

This connection that is assumed between the need of assistance and some form of personal depravity or shortcoming appears, superficially at least, to have much justification when we are considering the outcast, the criminal, and the extreme type of parasitic dependent. Here, apparently, the effects of evil and undisciplined living are so plain that no one may miss them. Reasoning from cause to effect in such cases seems an easy and simple process. We may see plainly in the very countenance the effects of vice, of intemperance, of cringing helpless dependency. From this very elementary reading of character, and reasoning from effect to cause, we imagine that we rise to the perception of the earlier, subtler, less easily recognizable evidences of other faults and evil tendencies which, if unchecked, lead to the more deplorable conditions. We discover, or think we discover, that unemployment is the first step toward vagrancy; that poverty in which there are no discernible signs of degeneration is an intermediate stage between independence and pauperism; that suffering and privation naturally attendant upon widowhood, orphanage, acute illness, or friendless old age, are suspicious circumstances, justifying disciplinary measures even though also demanding palliative relief; and finally, that every application for charitable assistance, for what-

POVERTY AND MALADJUSTMENT

ever reason made, is to be looked upon as the occasion, not for lightening the burden of the one who asks aid, but for being sure that the burden is heavy enough for the discipline which is assumed, as a matter of course, to be required. This attitude, it is obvious, is one which is natural for high-minded, conscientious, and intelligent persons. It rests upon an inability to trust human nature under generous treatment, and yet it may have no trace of smug hypocrisy. On the contrary, it may represent a high degree of personal responsibility, a genuine concern for the more permanent welfare of those who are in trouble, and steadfast determination not to do anything that will injure the character of another, even though at the request of that other himself. It may even be compatible with a sympathetic and considerate attitude. It may represent a desire to consider the souls rather than merely the bodies of the poor. I have come to believe, nevertheless, after some years of careful, candid, and open-minded consideration of the subject, that this entire view of poverty is one which rests upon an unproved and unfounded assumption.

The only thing that we are warranted in taking for granted when a family asks for assistance is that they believe themselves to be in need of assistance. They may be right or wrong about the fact; they may have

MISERY AND ITS CAUSES

very imperfect notions as to where their assistance should come from, if they do require it; they may wofully underestimate or overestimate the amount of assistance that they require; they may be totally unable to give any clear and consistent account of the reasons why they require it. If, however, they are not mistaken about the fact and are really in need, and if they have come to an appropriate place to ask for it, it is fair and reasonable that nothing whatever should be taken for granted except the need which has been revealed by the application.

III

In contrast with the idea that misery is moral, the inexorable visitation of punishment for immoral actions and the inevitable outcome of depraved character, I wish to present the idea that it is economic, the result of maladjustment, that defective personality is only a halfway explanation, which itself results directly from conditions which society may largely control.

The question which I raise is whether the wretched poor, the poor who suffer in their poverty, are poor because they are shiftless, because they are undisciplined, because they drink, because they steal, because they have superfluous children, because of personal depravity, personal inclination, and natural preference; or whether they are shiftless and undisciplined and drink and steal and are unable to care for their too numerous children because our social institutions and economic arrangements are at fault. I hold that personal depravity is as foreign to any sound theory of the hardships of our modern poor as witchcraft or demoniacal possession; that these hardships are economic, social, transitional, measurable, manageable. Misery, as we say of tuberculosis, is communicable, curable, and preventable. It lies not in the unalterable nature of things, but in our particular human institutions, our social arrangements, our tenements and streets and subways, our laws and courts and jails, our religion, our education, our philanthropy, our politics, our industry and our business.

The difference between the misery of the Inferno and the misery of New York is not so much one of degree. Men and women and children here suffer, if not so much as in hell, at least to the full limit of their human capacity. It is not in its diversity. There are more kinds of misery in New York than Milton ever dreamed of in his blindness.

The real difference is that at which I have hinted — that the one is presented as moral, appropriate to the individual character, and therefore utterly hopeless. The other is economic, accidental, and transfigured by the abiding presence of hope. The one is a chief ornament of hell — considering its purpose and character. The other is a chief blight upon earth — considering its purpose and character. The one remains, for it is an integral part of the conception of the region in which it is placed. The other cannot remain, for it is irreconcilable with the conception of the society upon which it is an excrescence; or if in

POVERTY AND MALADJUSTMENT

the mysteries of God it is reconcilable, yet only in the sense that it is here for us to overcome, yielding its mysterious blessing only as we become wise enough, and strong enough, and good enough to destroy it.

No doubt we do encounter instances in which in this life individuals who suffer are but paying penalties of their own misdeeds. Passion and indolence do have their consequences. I have no quarrel with those who seek through education in the family, in church, in school, or in neighborly relations, to instil in young and old a wholesome fear of consequences. Nature teaches us in lessons written large in human experience that certain habits will eventually prove injurious and other habits salutary. We are fully warranted in taking these lessons to heart and passing them on to such as are not fools, and therefore do not insist on learning in the dearest of all schools, that of experience.

It is the reverse of this position that is not tenable. Evil passions and indolence produce misery, but it does not follow that misery, all misery, or most misery, is to be attributed to indolence or evil passions. The position which I suggest for your consideration is merely that there is no presumption of wrong-doing in the misery of the poor, that it may not be disciplinary, that it may not be punishment, that it may not be the working out of moral character. It may indeed be

MISERY AND ITS CAUSES

any of these things in a given instance, but the burden of proof is upon those who allege it, and no charitable society is justified, no public relief agency or institution is justified, in basing its policies upon the assumption that because these men before us are afflicted in mind or body, therefore either they or their parents have sinned.

IV

It is essential that we should make another distinction — the distinction between this misery of the poor and genuine poverty. There are indeed hardships and deprivations which are associated with poverty. Ireland has known them, when, in Elizabeth's reign, thirty thousand persons are said to have perished in a single year, chiefly from starvation; and when again, in Victoria's reign, vast numbers of the Irish people in sorrow and homesickness abandoned the green isle and sought new homes, where with pick and spade, with hod and barrow, they helped to build the industries of other lands.

Spain has known real poverty, when, at the close of Philip's disastrous reign, the Armada destroyed, the expensive wars ended, the industrious Moors expelled, the mines over sea exhausted, and the peninsula thrown back upon her own resources, it was found that those resources were meagre and that the people were poor. In striking contrast with what happened in that period, just four centuries ago, we have seen Spain in our time

MISERY AND ITS CAUSES

actually benefited by defeats which, from a military point of view, were equally striking, and by the loss in the nineteenth century of the last remnants of that colonial empire which she built up in the sixteenth. In her withdrawal from the responsibilities of government in the islands she left poverty, genuine poverty, as the most notable of her parting gifts. This also is changing, but ten years ago Cuba and Porto Rico and the Philippines had more of poverty than all continental United States.

Italy has known poverty in this literal and original sense. Although four millions of Victor Emmanuel's subjects have permanently expatriated themselves, although for eight years more than half a million a year have emigrated, the population of the peninsula has not diminished as did the population of Ireland in the last century, but rather it has increased. In proportion to resources there is still over-population. Living conditions in many districts are described as similar to those of the Middle Ages.[1] When the districts which are now virtually abandoned because of malaria are again available, and when by changes in her laws and customs the able-bodied men between seventeen

[1] Antonio Mangano: The Effect of Emigration upon Italy. In *Charities and the Commons*, XIX, 1329, 1475; XX, 13, 167, 323.

POVERTY AND MALADJUSTMENT

and forty years of age, who constitute three-fourths of her emigration, are induced or enabled to stay at home and are put at profitable work, there may be other relief from their poverty than that which emigration with all its disadvantages has to offer. But as it now stands, especially in the southern provinces, there are to be found appalling evidences of misery due to mere inability to produce enough of the necessities of life. The recent devastation of the earthquake, like the horrible Black Death which in the fourteenth century swept away half of the population of England, may come in time to be looked upon as a blessing in disguise — a very heavy and forbidding disguise, I admit. From these poorest provinces alone there have been swept away nearly half as many people as have ordinarily emigrated from the whole of Italy in a year; and, unlike the emigration process, the earthquake has taken the aged, the feeble, the young, the helpless, along with the rest, and not, in disproportionate numbers, the able-bodied men of working years.

I do not propose earthquakes as a remedy for distress, although over-population is clearly an evil, and although the experience of San Francisco shows that an enormous destruction of property may have comparatively little effect on the standards of living and

MISERY AND ITS CAUSES

the apparent prosperity of the community in which it occurs.

Such poverty as that of Ireland, of Spain, of Italy, and of agricultural Russia, is not entirely unknown in America also. In New England, on the frontier, in southern mountains, in deserted mining regions, even in the backward districts of our own Empire State, you find deep local traces of it. You find here and there, in every country, spots where food is scarce, where human wants are unsupplied for the reason that nature is niggardly and capital is scarce. Labor is of little value and wages are low for the reason that there is no profitable employment for labor. This is poverty. It is to be found ordinarily in primitive, agricultural communities rather than in industrial centres. It is a condition from which mankind struggles upward by uneven stages, sometimes very rapidly, when nature grows lavish or invention forges new implements; sometimes very slowly, when natural resources fail and civilization is stagnant.

Even the possession of great natural resources, such as deposits of iron and coal and the precious metals, or a rich soil, or luxuriant vegetation, or a splendid harbor, does not of itself insure a community against real poverty. Until invention has shown the way to apply labor to such resources they are no safeguard

POVERTY AND MALADJUSTMENT

against poverty. Until the wants of men have been adjusted to the utilization of resources they are as if they were not. Tropical regions are called naturally productive, but they are rather the natural home of poverty, through all the ages, until there is secured an adjustment between wants and industries based upon the utilization of resources.

V

The short and simple annals of the poor have spoken eloquently of poverty of resources. The traditional worthy poor of whom we hear in poetry and in exhortation have been poor because toil is unproductive, because their labor is expended at the margin of production, as economists say, where a day's work yields but a meagre return.

The annals of the city's tenements to-day have little to say of poverty of resources. They are neither short nor simple. They speak more eloquently and more tragically than the traditional annals of the poor; even more eloquently and more tragically, as I have already hinted, than the blank verse in which poets have described the sufferings of departed spirits. But the story which they tell is not of poverty, even as it is not of punishment. It is in the main of social maladjustment. It is in the main of adverse conditions over which the individual who suffers is unable to exercise effective control but which are not beyond social control.

Here again I can bring you instances which might be deemed convincing evidence to the contrary. There

POVERTY AND MALADJUSTMENT

are individuals who do survive and who do triumph over the most adverse conditions. No man can set bounds to the capacity of the individual human spirit even when chained to a frail body. Indomitable courage, superhuman strength of will, inexhaustible persistence, ingenuity and invention, called forth by necessity, if not, as the old proverb teaches, the very child of necessity, are qualities that we do meet in everyday life, and thanks to such qualities the exceptional individual wrests victory from the teeth of disaster.

It is hard to tell how much a man can stand. You recall a recent incident of a laborer employed in the East River Tunnel who discovered a tiny leak in the roof of the air chamber in which, under the great air pressure incident to such tunnelling, he was at work. He tried to stop it, but the hole grew rapidly larger, not because water was coming in, but because air was escaping. Into the hole made in this way in the roof of the tunnel the man himself was finally driven by the force of the compressed air and up through the mud and sand of the bed of the river and through the river itself into the air above, very much to the astonishment of the crew of a tug-boat who had the honor of rescuing a man thrown into the river from an altogether different direction from what is customary. The workman survived this extraordinary experience, going to the hospital rather as a matter of form than because he felt it to be necessary, and complaining next day, as he told the story to his associates, of a little stiffness but of no serious consequences.

A surgeon tells of a soldier wounded in the Philippines by a bullet which passed clear through the skull, leaving it apparently in the condition of a crushed eggshell. Without any extraordinary surgical attention the wounds healed successfully and here again there were no serious permanent consequences. Such things happen. Nevertheless, most of us would prefer not to take the chance of a wound like the soldier's or an ascent like the tunnel laborer's.

Having exceptional instances in mind a worker among the poor may not unnaturally attribute to moral weakness the failure of any family to cope successfully with such adversities as it encounters. It depends upon the standards which one applies. If we are to say that weakness of character is responsible for the failure of any individual to overcome obstacles which Columbus or Darwin or Lincoln would have overcome, then we do but set up a wholly unreasonable standard, useless for practical purposes, even though we do find here and there unrecorded village Hampdens, mute, inglorious Miltons, who would measure up to it.

POVERTY AND MALADJUSTMENT

We have no right to demand that the poor shall meet single-handed, as stray heroes have done, adverse conditions to which ordinary average human beings are not, as a matter of fact, ordinarily subjected. It may even be that the qualities that have caused the successful to survive and to overcome will not always bear close scrutiny. Cunning, rather than strength of character, insensibility rather than patience, the physical endurance of an animal nature rather than the higher and more complex spiritual organization of a fully civilized man, conformity to vice rather than superior virtue, may account for the better showing of the successful in the economic struggle, which is only in part as yet a moral struggle. Let us hesitate to praise indiscriminately the great and the powerful, or even the merely successful and prosperous, until we have so far developed a civic conscience, and so far socialized business and industry, as well as the refined arts, that cunning and brute force no longer obtain the natural rewards of right living and genuine service to mankind.

VI

We now turn to the misery of our own day and our own community — the surplus misery, as I have called it, which we are all concerned to reduce and so far as we can to eliminate, and which is of such a nature as to constitute a social, not merely an individual, problem. If it is not to any appreciable extent poverty of national or community resources, as it clearly is not; if it is not merely the natural result of personal depravity, as I believe that it is not, — what is its nature? What are its several embodiments, to which we may look for some indications of its character and its causes?

First, then, the one thousand men and women in Greater New York who last year took their own lives, the seven thousand in the registration area of the United States who in the year 1908 took their own lives, are clearly an indication of human misery.

True, suicide may often be, as the verdicts so often declare, but a manifestation of temporary insanity; but insanity itself is a phase of misery, of which suicide, when it is due to insanity, is only one, and one of the least important, manifestations. Suicide is not excep-

POVERTY AND MALADJUSTMENT

tionally common among the poor. It occurs among them, but also, as we well know, among university professors, bank presidents, and in other ranks of society. I have heard the pastor of a metropolitan church, three of whose parishioners had committed suicide, preach bravely upon the sanctity of life, and urge upon his people, who were far above the average in intelligence, the elementary duty of remaining alive, even though in humiliation or in pain. I am not here concerned with the personal cowardice, or the incredible folly, or the egregious selfishness of the typical suicide. I am not discussing with the philosophers whether there may be extreme instances, as, for example, of painful and incurable malady in advanced life, when suicide can be theoretically defended. I have rather to consider whether the misery of which the act itself is in the vast majority of cases certainly a symptom, is ordinarily from poverty, from deprivation of the necessaries of life; whether, again, it can be traced to personal delinquencies of the individual who gives such irrefutable evidence of his despair; or whether it is a result of maladjustment.

Three years ago the Joint Application Bureau made an experimental inquiry into forty-three cases of unsuccessful attempts at suicide resulting in commitment to Bellevue Hospital. Nearly all of these patients were found to be self-supporting or to have friends and relatives who could have provided for their needs. This indicates that poverty plays little part as a cause of attempt at suicide, which does not, however, exclude the possibility that suicides in many instances are in need of aid and advice.[1]

The most obvious fact about the suicidal mania is its extraordinary increase in nearly all civilized countries — the rate of suicide having increased even while the general mortality rate has gone down. In the forty-three years since the establishment of our Health Department, the annual number of suicides in the old New York City, Manhattan and Bronx Boroughs, has increased tenfold. (Diagram 1.) There have been minor fluctuations attributable doubtless to industrial crises and similar causes, but any year which shows an exceptionally high number for such reasons, as for example 1874 and 1884, is soon surpassed by the regular annual increase which goes steadily on in periods of prosperity as in periods of depression. In 1905, 1906, and the first three quarters of 1907, the number of suicides was unusually low, but a great increase began at the time of the financial troubles in October, 1907, and the year 1908 showed an increase of fifty per cent over any of the preceding three years,

[1] O. F. Lewis. In *Charities and the Commons*, XVIII, 80.

POVERTY AND MALADJUSTMENT

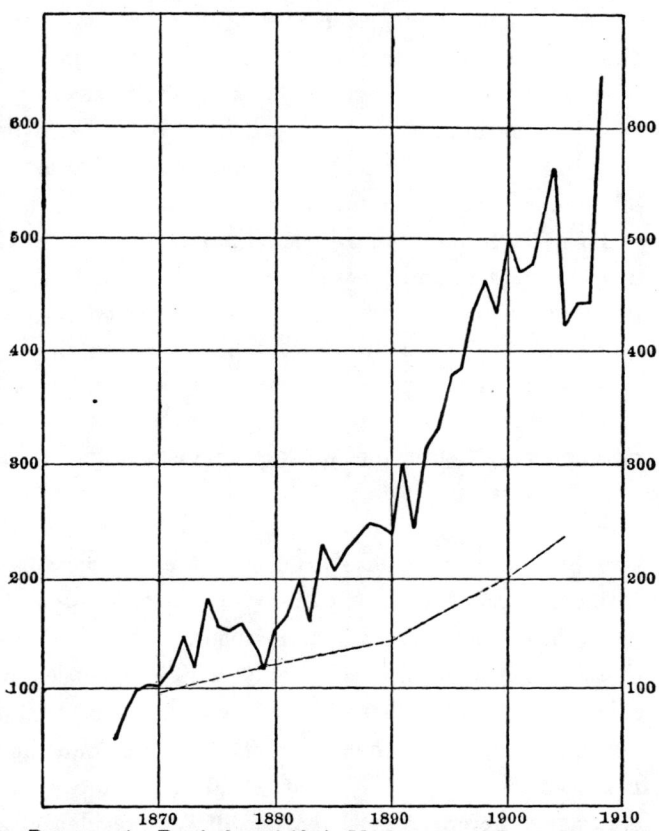

DIAGRAM 1. Deaths by suicide in Manhattan and Bronx Boroughs, 1866–1908. (Annual reports of the Department of Health of the City of New York for 1904 and successive years.)

The dotted line indicates, on a much smaller scale (1,000,000 population to 100 suicides), the population of the two boroughs at the census years.

[27]

a record higher by 77 than that of any previous year. Besides the 644 actual deaths from suicide in that year in the two boroughs, 235 cases of unsuccessful suicide were admitted to the prison ward at Bellevue Hospital — not of course by any means a full measure of the unsuccessful attempts.

This steady increase over a period of forty years of constantly augmenting wealth and enlightenment, an increase far in excess of the increase in population, but corresponding generally to what has occurred in European countries, appears to me to be a phenomenon of maladjustment, rather than of poverty or of depravity. No doubt the weakening of religious faith and the lessening of moral restraints often, perhaps usually, precede, in the individual, the act of self-slaughter, but these also are in part a result of the maladjustments to which I refer. Disease, disappointment, business failure, unemployment, and sheer loneliness are among the commonly assigned causes of suicide, but behind these, if we knew the facts, would we not usually find that the unfortunate suicide had not been rightly placed; that a different set of associates, a different occupation, a different residence, a different and generally not an impossible adjustment of social or industrial relations, might have averted the catastrophe?

POVERTY AND MALADJUSTMENT

Statistics have shown that there are relations between suicide and many other natural and social phenomena.[1] The rate is higher in cities than in rural communities. Three or four men resort to suicide for every woman. The age at which the maximum number occurs is the decade between fifty and sixty. This advanced age is the more striking when we remember that in proportion to population the ratio would be still higher. In other words, if we consider not the absolute number, but the relation to population, the rate of suicide increases with every decade from under twenty to over seventy, thus controverting the popular impression as to the relatively large number of youthful suicides. They are most frequent in the spring and early summer months, suggesting that the nervous system does not adjust itself promptly to changes in atmospheric conditions. The hours most frequently chosen are not those of the silent and lonely night, but from six in the morning to three in the afternoon, hours of activity and noise and social intercourse. Protestants have a higher rate than Catholics, Roman Catholics than Greek Catholics, Christians than Jews.

[1] See Morselli: Suicide. Ogle: Suicides in England and Wales; in *Journal of the Statistical Society of London*, XLIX, 101. Dewey: Statistics of Suicide in New England; in *Publications of the American Statistical Association*, June and September, 1892.

MISERY AND ITS CAUSES

Suicides have increased with the increase in culture and general education, and in a given country are apt to be more numerous in the sections which are best educated, as judged by the superficial and inconclusive test of ability to read or to sign the marriage register. This is no ground for indictment against education, but it suggests the importance of adjusting our educational system to the requirements of active life.

War and periods of economic disturbance are generally followed by an increase of suicide, although in the actual stress of war and revolution petty individual troubles are forgotten and there is a decrease.

There is a low rate among laborers and clergymen, a high rate in the other learned professions, among those who follow sedentary occupations, and among those whose callings have temptations to an intemperate mode of life. Ready access to instruments of self-destruction seems to increase the probability of suicide. Soldiers, for example, medical practitioners and chemists, according to the English tables, all have high rates. This theory finds support in our own experience in the frequency with which the elevated railways, the subways, and Niagara Falls are chosen as a means of suicide. There is, at least in England, a correspondence between suicide and the general death-rate which leads to the inference that conditions and habits

POVERTY AND MALADJUSTMENT

which conduce to general unhealthiness conduce also to self-destruction.

The conclusion reached by Morselli, the leading authority on the subject, is that suicide is an incident of maladjustment; in his own words, that "it is an effect of the struggle for existence and of human selection, which works according to the laws of evolution among civilized people." The cure which he proposes is "to develop in man the power of well-ordering sentiments and ideas by which to reach a certain aim in life; in short, to give force and energy to the moral character."

That also is the cure which I would propose, though it may be that I have a somewhat different idea from what was in his mind as to the means of bringing it about. Professor Patten, in a little volume now in press,[1] puts into a nugget of wisdom the means on which I would rely "to give force and energy to the moral character." He says: "We strengthen the will not by discipline, but by giving the conditions for normal growth. There is thus no specific remedy for a weak will nor for vice. The road from vice is the road to complete development. Other paths and all repression only changes its form."

The Roman Catholic confessional, the suicide

[1] Climax and Product.

bureau of the Salvation Army, and such recent developments in Protestant churches as are typified by what is known as the Emmanuel movement, have great possibilities of good in helping individuals past a crisis which they might not survive unaided. Private individuals have many an unrecognized opportunity to relieve such misery as tends towards suicide, merely by readjusting other individuals who, as employees, or as relatives, or as parishioners, or as patients, or as beneficiaries, or as neighbors, put themselves to some extent under the influence of the employer, or relative, or pastor, or physician, or visitor, or neighbor, as the case may be. All social policies which tend to lessen maladjustment — preventive medicine, improved housing, higher standards of living, greater steadiness of employment, the easier obtaining of loans on reasonable terms, and above all the development of rational recreation and amusements — will reduce the number of suicides, by reducing its inciting cause.

VII

Next after suicides, in the minds of most of us, as obviously wretched and plunged in misery, are the incarcerated criminals, the 81,772 adult prisoners confined on sentence in the 1333 civil prisons of the United States,[1] and the 23,034 children and young persons in the 93 reformatory institutions.[2] (Diagram 2.) The state of New York, with less than ten per cent of the population of the country, has twelve per cent of the incarcerated adult criminals, and twenty-five per cent of the inmates of institutions for juvenile delinquents.

In these convicted criminals we have admittedly a host of unadjusted men and women, who have committed some definite offence of which they have been found guilty in due process of law. There need be no mawkish sentimentality in their behalf. I do not hold them up before you as victims, in any exceptional

[1] Special Report of the United States Census Bureau: Prisoners and Juvenile Delinquents in Institutions, 1904.

[2] Not all of these twenty-three thousand had committed offences. The figure includes "persons between seven and twenty-one years of age committed to the custody of reformatory institutions by some lawfully constituted authority."

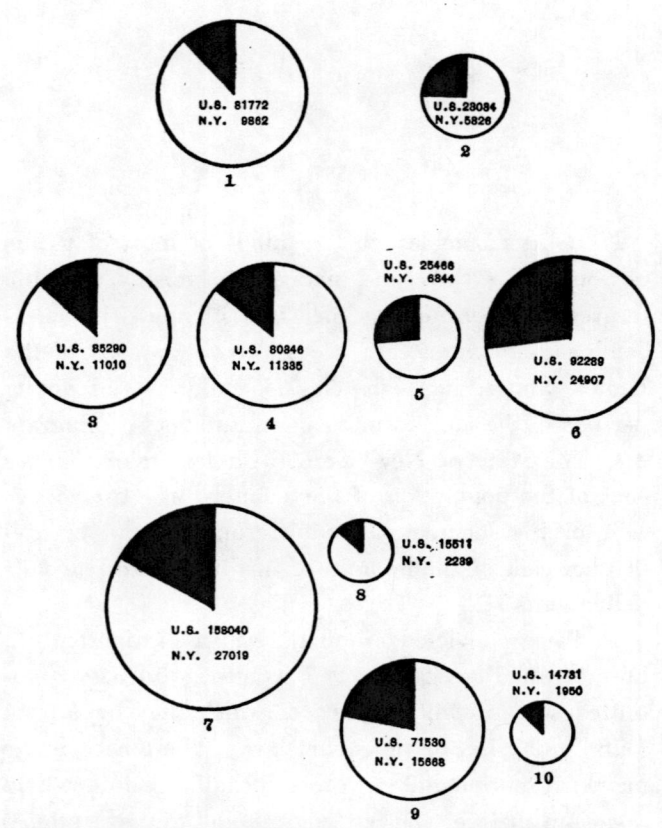

DIAGRAM 2. The institutional population of the United States on a given day in 1904.
1. In prisons. 2. In institutions for juvenile delinquents. 3. In almshouses. 4. In permanent homes for adults. 5. In temporary homes. 6. In orphanages and children's homes. 7. In institutions for the insane. 8. In institutions for the feeble-minded. 9. In hospitals. 10. In schools and homes for the deaf and blind.

The different circles represent, on the same scale for all, the total number of persons in the different classes of institutions, and the black portion the number in the state of New York.

[34]

POVERTY AND MALADJUSTMENT

degree, of social injustice. We are far too lenient with our criminals. We allow too many a crime to go unpunished, we imprison for too short a period, we pardon too easily, and we release after expiration of sentence arbitrarily, with no security against a repetition of the crime. And yet, a large part of the misery which leads straight to crime is clearly traceable to social failure. The responsibility of society for juvenile crime is so clearly recognized as to need no argument. The lack of play grounds, the defects of our system of elementary education, the evils associated with over-crowding in tenements, are among the failures of adjustment to present conditions which tend to the manufacture of youthful criminals; and after that process has once begun, the association of first offenders with hardened criminals, the futile system of definite short sentences, the absence of any comprehensive scheme of reformation and rehabilitation — though there are institutions and societies which do reform and rehabilitate, the inefficiency and corruption of criminal courts and police systems — though there are courts and police officers that are neither inefficient nor corrupt — speedily complete the process, so that the youthful offender, as he waxes in stature with the passing of the years, hardens also into an attitude of permanent hostility to society.

MISERY AND ITS CAUSES

This process is not a joyful one. On the contrary, it is fraught with misery, with hardships and suffering, with hatred and humiliation and revengeful resentment. All this might very often be changed. If those who are degenerate, really unfit for human companionship, were humanely but firmly segregated in suitable homes or colonies; if those who are really at war with society in spirit, however trivial their specific offence, were kept under discipline and educational training until they were reconciled; if those who, under the pressure of some extraordinary external impulse which is not likely to recur, have committed a crime, let us say against property, which they are ready to expiate by restitution, were treated by a method appropriate to their offence, and if an opportunity were given them on comparatively easy terms to regain an honorable place in society; if to those who are not criminals at all in any real sense, but who have fallen under the influence of evil associates, a chance were given under probation, — real probation, with so much of stern compulsion as is necessary to enforce compliance with rational conditions imposed by the court, and so much of human sympathy and understanding as will induce a disposition to comply with them, — we might arrest this downward career in many an individual. In fact, we do so arrest it now,

POVERTY AND MALADJUSTMENT

in so far as we have already transformed piecemeal our antiquated penal system. Social defence, relying chiefly upon reformation and the improvement of social conditions as its methods, has been accepted, though not yet altogether consciously, as the basis of our treatment of crime. Juvenile court, probation, reformatory, indeterminate sentence, prisoners' aid, and the industrial colony, are so many indestructible parts of a new and better plan which we shall one day piece together into an integral social police and correctional system — such a system as that to which Mrs. Lowell, inspired by a vision not yet realized, looked forward when she projected a great municipal department on the reduction of crime: to include prisons, reformatories, courts, police, and all the other agencies by which society would seek to extirpate crime rather than repress it; to educate, train, and reform the criminal rather than punish him; to promote justice and social order rather than perpetuate the misery from which crime naturally springs.

VIII

Even more repulsive to our eyes than the lifeless suicide, or the imprisoned murderer or thief, is that "unhappy being," if I may use words of Lecky, the historian of European morals, "whose very name is a shame to speak; who counterfeits with a cold heart the transports of affection, and submits herself as a passive instrument of lust; who is scorned and insulted as the vilest of her sex, and doomed, for the most part, to disease and abject wretchedness and an early death." "On that one degraded and ignoble form," he says, "are concentrated the passions that might have filled the world with shame. She remains, while creeds and civilizations rise and fall, the eternal priestess of humanity, blasted for the sins of the people."

Although these words do not paint too darkly the position of the prostitute, they fail to give an adequate idea of the full sweep of the misery which is associated with sexual immorality. I asked a probation officer the other day, who works daily and nightly with the unfortunate women brought into court on a charge of disorderly conduct, how much of the misery of

POVERTY AND MALADJUSTMENT

New York is, in her judgment, due to this cause alone, and she said, "Oh, nine-tenths of it." That was not a well-considered answer, and on cross-examination she would not insist upon her estimate, but it indicates a better perspective than the impatient dismissal of the whole subject which is the temptation of the average citizen, and it suggests the wider range which we must give our inquiry into the causes and consequences of this social phenomenon.

I believe Lecky to be entirely mistaken as to the essential nature of prostitution. Vice is not, as the quotation suggests, an external manifestation of one uncontrollable human impulse. When I see the evidences of deliberate commercial investment in the music halls, the dance halls, the Raines Law Hotels, and the saloons that encourage this social evil; when I learn of the corrupt alliance between politicians and policemen and vice; when I consider the savings by merchants and manufacturers who pay girls less than a living wage; when I consider the failure to give natural, normal, obviously essential oversight to girls in the period in which they most need protection, and the failure to give sound instruction to the youth of either sex on matters so vital to their own safety and the safeguarding of the race, — I have but scant patience with the theory of vice which calls for "a priestess of humanity," who at the same time, as Lecky puts it again, is "herself the supreme type of vice," and yet ultimately the most efficient guardian of virtue. Except in the case of a few moral perverts, girls become prostitutes in New York, not because of some mysterious and unalterable law of human nature, not because humanity demands a priestess; but because it is profitable for some people to perpetuate the existence of vicious resorts and places of amusements, because the difference between three dollars a week and twenty dollars a night is too great a temptation for a girl of weak will without a guardian, because the girls are neither watched when they are in danger nor taught when they are in ignorance, because children are not kept away from dangerous places, because again prostitution is not successfully kept out of the tenements, because working girls, when temporarily unemployed, have before their eyes the flaunting evidences of immoral prosperity, because girls who live in furnished rooms and boarding places have no place to receive their company except in their sleeping rooms, because of the privations that under-employment or irregular employment or underpaid employment or unemployment occasion, because of seasonal work and of work under bad conditions. Such social and economic causes as these do not account for all immorality — it

POVERTY AND MALADJUSTMENT

is not my province to account for all immorality, but rather to point out some of those adverse conditions from which immorality, like crime and self-destruction, are likely to result and in fact do result.

When I consider how those who do set out to deal seriously with the social evil persistently revert to the utterly discredited and futile method of licensing and segregating and sanctioning the evil instead of eradicating it, and to the inherently unjust and outrageous discrimination against the female prostitute, with virtual immunity for the male cadet who lives upon her earnings, and complete immunity for the male customer to whose demand she caters, I long for the rise of a prophet who will be able to open the eyes of the people to the simple elementary truth in this whole matter. There is but one truth, and it is simple. That truth is that purity of life is the only cure for the social evil. Until the churches and the schools, the public journals and the public platforms, the family physician and parents in the home, are free to teach and preach this truth, there will be no end of the social evil. That teaching is positive, and not negative. It has to do with health and vigor and the perpetuation of the race, not with vice, and disease, and ugliness, and death. That teaching is obstructed and thwarted by two things; by false modesty, and by greed. Those are the two maladjustments which stand in our way. The essential evil, towards which we should direct our attention, lies not in the residuum of vice which would remain because of the ultimate, ineradicable human passions for which public prostitution, in Lecky's conception of the matter, provides a safety-valve. The evil lies in the ignorance and in the habits to which we give tacit approval; against which we do not strive earnestly and openly and aggressively; concerning which there is a lamentable "conspiracy of silence." These evils are definite, quite within the grasp of any average intellect, and eradicable.

IX

After suicides and criminals and prostitutes we come, in our search for the embodiments of misery, to the institutions which have grown up to care for particular classes of dependents. All of these are naturally brought under suspicion as the peculiar abodes of misery. Each specialized group holds in precipitation, as a chemist might say, one of the well-recognized causes of human misery: physical disability in the hospitals; permanent physical defect in schools and homes for deaf and blind; mental disease and deficiency in the institutions for the insane and feeble-minded; friendless old age in the public almshouses and in the private homes for the aged; homeless childhood in the orphan asylums; immorality in the temporary homes for women; lack of work in the temporary homes for men.

There were 85,290 persons in the almshouses of the United States on January 1, 1905, and 80,346 more in the permanent homes for adults, most of which are privately managed homes for the aged or for incurables. (Diagram 2.) In the orphanages and homes for children there were 92,289; in municipal lodging houses and other temporary homes 25,466,[1] — altogether considerably more than a quarter of a million of men, women and children, who, whatever other characteristics they may have, however widely they may differ from one another as individuals, have this in common, that they are not living in families, under the normal conditions of home life. To a great extent they are friendless. To be out of friends because one has outlived them, or for any other reason, is misfortune indeed.

On the same day there were in special institutions 158,040 insane and 15,511 feeble-minded; a large proportion, probably, of all the recognizably insane in our population, but a shamefully insignificant proportion of all the feeble-minded. The misery which they represent is not borne to any extent by themselves, but by their families, and in the case of the feeble-minded, discredit and unnecessary burdens rest upon the whole nation until we adopt a more enlightened policy. They are themselves, to a very great extent, the results of social neglect or social mismanagement.

On the same day there were 14,731 persons in the schools and homes for the deaf and the blind, who may

[1] For these and following figures about the institutional population, see the Special Reports of the United States Census Bureau on Paupers in Almshouses, Benevolent Institutions, Insane and Feeble-Minded in Hospitals and Institutions.

POVERTY AND MALADJUSTMENT

be taken as merely typifying the misery that is due to physical defect. These 14,731 are for the most part not personally unhappy; they are a small proportion of all the deaf and blind in our country — less than ten per cent [1] — and they are as a class the most fortunate portion. I mention them only because they are the only segregated group we have who suggest the misery that is due to those imperfect senses, those mutilated and deformed bodies, which are in every case a social and an economic handicap, and in the case of those who cannot be tenderly cherished and surrounded with compensations, one of the most cruel of adverse conditions.

In the hospitals, finally, there were on January 1, 1905, 71,530 persons suffering from disease or serious accident. This also is a small proportion of the total number who were sick on that day, — perhaps three per cent,[2] — though it is three times as many as there were in hospitals fifteen years before. This increase of two hundred per cent is an index not only of misfortune but also of humanity. It is of course no indication of an increase in the amount of sickness. It points rather to readjustment by which the sick are cared for in a more

[1] Based on the figures given in the Census Bureau report on the deaf and blind in the population in 1900.
[2] Based on an estimate arrived at by using Farr's ratio of morbidity to mortality.

MISERY AND ITS CAUSES

humane and intelligent way; in the manner recommended centuries ago by Sir Thomas More in his Utopia, where in his enlightened city one may, if he likes, be sick at home instead of using a public institution, but to do so is a serious error of judgment. Our figures include some who were in hospitals, not from necessity, but because there is a growing preference, among those who are able to pay for any medical or surgical care they may need, to be sick in a hospital rather than at home. The hospital population does concretely represent that large volume of misery which is due to disease and accident.

In the state of New York, with nine and one-half per cent of the population of the country, we have thirteen per cent of the inmates of schools and homes for the deaf and blind, thirteen per cent of the paupers in almshouses, fourteen per cent of the adults in permanent homes, fourteen per cent of the feeble-minded in institutions, seventeen per cent of the insane in special institutions, twenty-two per cent of the sick in hospitals, twenty-seven per cent of the inmates of temporary homes, and twenty-seven per cent of the children in orphanages and homes. Some of these high percentages are much to our credit, others are not; but none of them is an indication of the relative strength in our population of that particular class of dependents, and

POVERTY AND MALADJUSTMENT

such comparisons must always take into account the situation of New York City as the chief port of immigration, and its other exceptional conditions.

There is one more fairly well-defined group to be considered. It is outside of all these institutions and constitutes an institution of itself. I refer to the bread line. For the most part its individual units have had or will have experience on the inside of prison and hospital and almshouse and temporary shelter, but the bread line itself is an embodiment of misery more dire and unrelieved than is found in almost any other quarter. Out of health, out of work, out of friends, out of step with industry, out of touch with society, the men in the bread lines are not unfairly taken as the clearest and most unmistakable of all evidences of maladjustment.

I do not wish to represent that we find in these institutions, whether almshouse or hospital or asylum, such unbroken and universal misery, such constant depression of spirits, such universal resentment against fate, as may easily be imagined by those who have not been accustomed to walk their corridors and to sit by their bedsides. We may even look in vain for such outward tokens of misery among criminals and outcast women, though there is certainly little real joy among them. All of these groups combined do not exhibit by any means the sum of human misery, but each of them is

MISERY AND ITS CAUSES

an index of hardship and misfortune, even though individuals among them may not be miserable and others may be unconscious of their real misery, and others may indeed be able to excite admiration and envy by compensating qualities of mind and soul.

The causes of friendless old age, of orphanage, of physical and mental disease and defect, are many and intricate. Some of it is due, no doubt, to defective personality, physical and moral. Much of it, certainly, is the direct result of remediable social conditions, maladjustments which can be corrected. Children are left fatherless or motherless by the premature death of their parents from preventable disease; people come to old age, frequently an early old age, disabled by overwork or work under bad conditions, having had little opportunity to make provision for age, or to bring up their children to a position in which they can care for their parents; much of the blindness is due to preventable causes; much of the feeble-mindedness to lack of custodial care for feeble-minded and epileptic women and men; some of the accidents to unguarded machinery; much of the illness to unsanitary conditions of home and factory and to a low standard of living imposed by a low rate of wages. Thus much of the misery which the institutional population reflects certainly represents a defective social economy.

X

The thesis which I have maintained is that not poverty and not punishment explains the misery of our modern commercial and industrial communities, but rather social maladjustment. It will not, I trust, be inferred that I would give aid or countenance to those who with rash or violent hand would destroy the foundations on which mankind has begun to rear the structure of civilization. The institutions which have come into being, not by distinct and deliberate legislative enactments, but by the slow evolutionary processes of natural selection, and by the no less evolutionary and natural processes of the development of law and custom, are of far more significance and value to us all than any artificial, suddenly created mechanism which we are likely to invent. The family, the state, the church, property, the civil and the criminal law, courts of justice, free exchange of goods and of services, contract, the ballot, public education, public relief, democracy, the rule of the people with standards, which G. Lowes Dickinson[1] distinguishes from ochlocracy, or the rule of the mob without

[1] Justice and Liberty.

standards, — these great social institutions I would not overthrow if I could. No revolutionists could overthrow them if they would. When I seek, with absolute frankness, and a very earnest desire to see things as they are, the causes of misery here in the city of New York, I have no more intention of challenging the basis of our society, of our industry, of our civilization, than the physician intends to challenge the laws of anatomy and physiology when he looks upon disease. I seek but to express vividly and concretely, as we social workers find them, the conditions which appear to us naturally and inevitably favorable to the perpetuation and increase of human misery. If there shall emerge from the gloomy picture the brighter outlines of a social programme that satisfies our sense of justice, so much the better.

CHAPTER II

OUT OF HEALTH

I

IN the homes of the poor we come closer to the causes of misery than in hospital or almshouse, in orphan asylum or prison, in night court or bread line or coroner's office. In the homes of the poor we find the beginnings of those tendencies which in the exceptional cases lead to suicide or crime, to disabling disease and helplessness, to friendlessness and public dependence, but which in vastly more cases do not reach those extreme stages, though they lead ever in those directions.

We find not merely the beginnings, but the unfolding and interaction of all these tendencies, affecting individuals as in the institutional populations, and affecting also the welfare of families. In the homes of the poor we find the dire consequences of death and disease, of unemployment and under-employment, of overwork and nervous strain, of dark and ill-ventilated and overcrowded rooms, of under-nourishment and exposure and poisoned food, of ignorance and maladjustment. In the homes of the poor, we find hardships and burdens not unlike those which we find also in the homes of the prosperous and well-to-do. We find also courage and patience and charity. We find extraordinary resources and extraordinary powers of resistance. Again I find it difficult, as always, to generalize about the poor without falling straightway into contradictions and paradoxes, and so I say simply that we find in the homes of the poor much misery which is not true poverty and not punishment, misery which is but a part of our common heritage, a part of the result of a common failure in which they vicariously suffer for the sins of others, a part of a common burden which we may bear in common if we so desire.

Ill health is perhaps the most constant of the attendants of poverty. It has been customary to say that twenty-five per cent of the distress known to charitable societies is caused by sickness. An inquiry into the physical condition of the members of the families that ask for aid, without for the moment taking any other complications into account, clearly indicates that whether it be the first cause or merely a complication from the effect of other causes, physical disability is at any rate a very serious disabling condition at the time of application in three-fourths — not one-fourth — of all the families that come under the care of the Charity Organization Society, who are probably in this respect in no degree exceptional among families in need of charitable aid.

OUT OF HEALTH

That we may see this disability in its natural human relations, I venture to introduce the discussion of ill health as a cause of misery with the stories of four families.

II

Our first family consists of an Irish laborer forty-two years of age, a Scotch wife ten years younger, and seven children. They came to this country four years ago, just after the man had failed in business through the foolish indorsement of another man's note. The wife's father is in fairly good circumstances in Scotland, but too much annoyed at his son-in-law's business incapacity to do anything for them. Putting the end of the story first, as all impatient readers prefer, I am happy to say that this man is now employed and supporting his family, and that his wife has undertaken to repay what money has been loaned to them within the past year. I fear, however, that this is temporary, unsubstantial prosperity, reflecting the buoyancy of hope, rather than that permanent relief which would justify such confidence.

Intelligent, willing, sober, and respectable they are, but not efficient and not able-bodied. When the wife first came for help a year ago her husband had been out of work for five months, with only now and then an

OUT OF HEALTH

occasional day's work. He was in need of a surgical operation. Twice the receivers of the Metropolitan Railway had given him a chance. Both times he was discharged within a month as incompetent. Later, after he had had his operation and recovered, he worked in the Woodyard, successfully as long as he was favored by light tasks, but unable to perform work of ordinary severity. Although he had recovered from his acute illness, strength, energy, and physical vigor did not appear. When he applied for work he was not taken on because he was obviously physically unfit. Even the Special Employment Bureau for the Handicapped could do little for him. Finally a superintendent of buildings in an educational institution, though with many misgivings, took him on where he is still employed, irregularly. So much for the man. The wife also is ill. She has at first some heart trouble, and neuralgia. At the same time the oldest child, twelve years of age, has to go to the hospital for a serious operation on her throat. These misfortunes are definitely reported on the day when the father is about to have his operation, and on the same day the mother expresses a fear that two of the younger children have measles, — a fear which in a day or two is confirmed. In another week still another child develops a very sore throat and the nurse reports that the baby has a sore mouth.

MISERY AND ITS CAUSES

When they have to move, a month later, because the agent objects to seven children, though he cannot dispossess them while they have the measles, the mother of seven solves the rent problem in a new apartment by taking in a boarder. It is a larger apartment of course — five rooms — and it costs seventeen dollars a month. Her own physical infirmities, however, have only just begun. Her leg is injured in an accident, boils follow, and it is three months before she is perceptibly better. Meantime the baby has been very ill and another child has had pneumonia.

At various times in this year's experience the visitor has reported that they seemed discouraged, each time, however, as if it were an unusual and rather surprising development, worthy to be noted on that account, and each time, if I recollect correctly, it was not the illness, or the adverse sudden stroke of fate that appeared to them discouraging, but rather its long sequelæ, the fact of not finding employment, the fact of not regaining strength, or the fact forsooth of not finding a real estate agent who wanted a janitress with seven children!

You will readily separate in this history the accidental from the typical. The large family, the multiplicity of children's diseases, the operations, the failure in business in the old country — these are the accidents of this particular case; but the physical incapacity directly

OUT OF HEALTH

resulting from disease and under-nourishment and the complications of the physical and social environment — these are typical and fundamental to our understanding of causes and remedies.

III

I turn to another case, in which for two years accident and illness have shaped the family history. The woman has become a widow within that period. She is now a cleaner in one of the district offices of the Charity Organization Society.

When she came from Ireland a girl of twenty-one, just twenty-five years ago, she went into service with a lady whose name she still gives as a reference and who writes as follows: "In regard to William and Nellie Brown, William worked in my husband's factory as a truckman. Nellie lived with me first as upstairs girl, then as cook. She was married from my house and I took her back again after her marriage to William. She lived with me for some time after her marriage. Nellie was always a good, honest, sober girl and kind to everyone. I am more than sorry to think there should have been made such a change in their lives. I know any help of any kind whatever will be well placed if given to Nellie and her family of little children."

That is all that any one could ask in the way of a character. It is fully confirmed by the investigation

OUT OF HEALTH

made at the time of application for aid. The rooms were clean and comfortable. The children were well cared for. The family physician, who had known them for twenty years and had treated them in all illness, corroborated in every particular such statements as had been made to us.

What now was the distressing change which had moved the pity of their old-time employers and which brought them to us, not, I must add again, on their own application, but on a neighbor's intervention? The trouble was that the sturdy truckman of forty-six was lying ill in the J. Hood Wright Memorial Hospital, suffering from injury to his spine, caused in part, or so his wife believed, by the heavy lifting which his employment required, though the official diagnosis says combined sclerosis and pernicious anæmia. After having been taken care of at home for ten weeks, until their savings were exhausted, he remained alive four months more in the hospital, and when he died he left just enough insurance on his life to give his body decent burial.

So we have a widow on our hands with four small children. She is no longer robust, however strong she may have been as a maid twenty years ago. She says that she has stomach trouble and the diagnosis of St. Luke's Hospital says gastric indigestion. She is janitress with free rent and a little besides. She is taking in washing — though she has various ailments from time to time besides her gastric indigestion; such as pleurisy and a bad cough. There was another member of the household, William's sister, of feeble intellect, with the enlarged head of the idiot, but able to give some help in the care of the children.

I shall not enter into the history of the relief, as I am attempting to describe conditions in this family and not the work of a district committee, but one feature of it is worthy of mention. William, twelve years of age, at work in violation of the law, was on the conscience of the committee. He was taking care of a telephone, his duties light, his employer interested in him, and the conditions favorable, with promise of promotion. His mother pleaded that he should not be disturbed. He had not been doing particularly well in school and he had never been so well, so good, and so happy as since he had begun to work. But the committee was obdurate on this point, seeing clearly its duty to uphold the law, and made its provision of a pension conditional on William's going to school. Just as this decision was reached, and before it had been communicated to the anxious mother, a neighbor called at the office with the startling news that William, this strong, happy, twelve-year-old youngster, had been hit by an automobile and had been taken badly injured to the very hospital where his father

OUT OF HEALTH

was still a patient. Into the details of the pitiful struggle of the next year and a half for health for the boy and for health for the mother, and relief for the idiotic aunt by surgical operation, of church relief, fresh air outings, and partial employment for the partially disabled woman and light employment for the boy, now also seriously disabled, perhaps for life, of the illegal, surreptitious substitution of the second boy, only ten years old, in the place which at the time of his accident William still held in spite of the law and in spite of the society, — into these details of her struggle against adverse conditions and her partial success, as I have said, I cannot enter.

I hold this story also, though but briefly sketched in outline, to be fairly typical of the conditions which cause the misery of the poor. So typical is it indeed, so much like the average, ordinary case, that when I asked the district agent under whose care she has been to tell me about some of her families, this one did not occur to her. She began to tell me about an exceptional case in which there had been an extraordinary combination of unfavorable misfortunes. "Wait," I said, before she had gone very far, "I don't want a story that is exceptional. Let me ask you on a venture about your own cleaner here in the district office. Probably she has been chosen, has she not, from among your applicants? Tell me about her."

MISERY AND ITS CAUSES

Rather reluctantly at first, until the details came into her mind, she told me about this more ordinary, more typical case. I submit it to your judgment, whether if it is typical it is not also very illuminating.

IV

In the two instances which I have cited misery is the result of ill health, disease, and death in families which are entitled to be called respectable families, in which there are no notable stains of misconduct upon the record, unless perchance the business failure of the accommodating Irishman is to be so described. But of course I would tell only half of my story and write myself down as a false interpreter of social conditions if I sought to give the impression that misery of the same sort is not often accompanied by lapses from the path of rectitude. It is not alone the good that die prematurely. It is not alone the striking or interesting case that illustrates social conditions. It is not alone the attractive family that requires our sympathetic understanding. It is not alone the native born and those who speak our language that suffer and need help.

A few days before Christmas, five years ago, an Italian woman came to the lower east side district office, from a day nursery, with her eleven-year-old daughter. Her husband had died four months before and since then she had tried to support herself and the three children by sewing at home. By working seventeen hours a day she could earn barely three dollars a week. The oldest child was Joseph, fourteen, out of school, running the streets and "worrying his mother a good deal." Francesca, the little girl of eleven, also out of school, " seemed bright and intelligent." She helped her mother sew, did all the washing, and was even found lighting a fire with some wood Joseph had picked up (and the room, the record adds, was full of smoke). Then there was Tony, a child of four, who apparently had brought them, *via* the day nursery, to the district office. The mother "looked delicate and not able to do very hard work."

They had been in New York four years. Their relatives in Italy were very poor. A brother of her husband with his family lived next door, on Forsythe Street. They had lived in the same house for a month but our family had been put out because the children made so much noise romping with their cousins. They had been put out of another house because they were entertaining two families of friends just come from Italy. The Laundry was suggested, but the mother said she could not go because she "got sick when she put her hands in water." A settlement asked Francesca to join a club of Italian girls, and tried, unsuccessfully, to get hold of Joseph. Francesca was told to come to the office in the morning, to be taken to school and properly started. But she did

OUT OF HEALTH

not come, she did not go to the settlement, and when the visitor went to see them, they had moved away, with the relatives from next door, no one knew where.

In October the mother came again with Fanny to the lower west side office. The two families were living together in three ten-dollar rooms, and the woman's seventeen-year-old brother had recently come from Italy and was living with them. He was "working at flowers" and making only $1.50 a week. Our widow was out of work. A settlement had got hold of the children and they were all in school, including Joseph, who was reluctantly and unsatisfactorily complying with the new child labor law. The mother did not want to go to the Laundry, but "finally consented." The next day came Fanny to say her mother had secured work at finishing pants, which was now her trade, and so she would not need to go to the Laundry. In December she was still working, but earning only about three dollars a week, "which," the record says, "she feels is insufficient for all her needs." While she could earn as much as that, however, she would not consider any other kind of work. The brother's earnings meantime had increased until he was paying two dollars a week for board. In January the settlement was "satisfied with present conditions," and the record was closed for the time being.

In less than a month a third settlement asked help for

the family. Joseph had not yet completed the required grade, and he was staying away from school. The truant officer could not find him and his mother would not tell where he was. It was reported that she had sent him "up to Fourteenth Street" to keep him out of school, that he gave her three dollars a week and "changed his employment often." Later he was placed in the Truant School, did well there, and in May got his working papers.

In the summer the friendly visitor sent Fanny to the country, and the next fall she was in school quite regularly. The mother's brother was making ten dollars a week during the rush season and Joseph was at home, working and giving his mother four dollars out of his wages of five. This fall of 1905 was the best time the family had seen since we had known them.

In December Fanny was not well. The friendly visitor sent her to the country, but the matron of the house said she was very wild. She came home and was entered at the Manhattan Trade School, on a scholarship, to learn machine operating. About this time Joseph began to steal from his mother, to stay away from home, and to frequent pool-rooms. In February he was arrested and sent to the reformatory on Hart's Island, where, as in the Truant School, he made a good record. The mother's brother, too, who generally paid five

OUT OF HEALTH

dollars a week, spent all his wages one week in the poolroom. Fanny did not do well at the Trade School, staying away a great deal.

In July our applicant was examined at the Board of Health Clinic and it was found that she had incipient tuberculosis. The medical report said her general condition was good, the prognosis favorable, and that she was able to work. She did go on working, earning now from ten to twelve dollars a week.

In October Fanny, not yet fifteen, was arrested for shoplifting and was sent to the Protectory. Joseph came back home about this time, but was doing nothing and was talking about going back to Italy. The incipient consumptive is described as "not in very good condition physically."

A year later, November, 1907, Fanny was at home again, working with her mother. Joseph was still at home, idle, and still talking about Italy. He was told that he must earn his passage money if he wanted to go.

The next spring they were found in one small room, the woman apparently out of work, Fanny earning $3.50 in a flower factory, Joseph working for a barber Saturdays and Sundays. A third time a Laundry permit was offered her and a third time she declined on the ground that she was not able to do that kind of work. The nurse took her again to the clinic of the Board of Health, with the same result as before. She came back after it and asked for a Laundry permit. The physician who examined her offered Fanny a position as chamber-maid in his family, which she refused because she would not stay away from home overnight. He also examined Fanny and found that she, too, had tuberculosis. The settlement just at this time offered the mother a position as maid, but she "did not want to be a servant to any one and would rather die than do that kind of work." In June she tried to commit little Tony, who has hardly been mentioned up to this time, to an institution as a public charge, but the application was not approved.

Fanny was sent to the state sanatorium. Her mother would not consider it for herself and probably could not have got in. She had a place at service in the country with Tony but she kept it only two days as "she was not satisfied." Joseph went back to Sicily, through the generosity of a relative, to his grandfather. In January, 1909, Fanny was still at Ray Brook and her mother was working "somewhere uptown," earning seven or eight dollars a week.

There you have, as you will have discovered, a record of overcrowding, of improper home work in a tenement, of seasonal work in factories, of lack of proper training for children, and of inadequate relief; but behind all these things, resulting perhaps in part from them, and

OUT OF HEALTH

causing them in part, you have widowhood and half orphanage, and you have physical disability, taking the very natural — almost inevitable — specific form of tuberculosis in both mother and daughter. You will notice that the boy, Joseph, did well both times under discipline — even under the discipline of the reformatory on Hart's Island. The girl, on the other hand, did not do well at the Trade School, and in fact was arrested for shoplifting at about the time she left that excellent institution. Perhaps she may have fallen in with a bad companion there, or perhaps she is one of those who do best in the atmosphere of the home. Except for this single instance, she has seemed to be all that could be desired, — affectionate, helpful, and industrious.

V

May I add one more story, much briefer, and of a far less attractive home? The man at the head of this family was a deaf-mute of grossly immoral habits and violent temper, but an excellent workman, both as engraver and photographer, and able to earn a good living. The woman was a second wife, in good repute among her neighbors, but of a very violent temper. She also, however, was intelligent and capable. She had married against the wishes of her parents, who were respectable working people in a Newfoundland town. There were two young girls (the man's children by a former wife, from whom he had secured a divorce in Oregon on account of her immorality) about whom conflicting stories were told. The neighbors and Sunday-school teacher, who had been interested in them for years, spoke of them both in the highest terms as industrious and of good morals (except that the older one was perhaps "unreliable"), and as giving of their earnings towards the support of a most unhappy home. The parents, on the other hand, gave a very unfavorable account of their conduct. The only child of the couple lived but

OUT OF HEALTH

a short time, and it was during that short life that care was given by the district committee on the solicitation of the family physician. Man and wife quarrelled constantly, separated on various occasions, and when the baby died, the home was practically dissolved, the two girls securing employment in families through the interest of the Sunday-school teacher, and the parents going into a furnished room.

Thus physical infirmity falls on the just and on the unjust, robbing the one of the comfort which their integrity of character would seem to deserve, and giving to the other the shield from severe condemnation which their defects of character might otherwise invite.

VI

Perfect health, full physical vigor, and overflowing animal spirits are much more rare among dependent families than the moral virtues. The prevalence of ill health is due in large part of course to ignorance and the continuous neglect of the elementary rules of personal hygiene. The health department and the public schools, physicians and social workers, cry aloud from the house-tops the value of fresh air; of simple, inexpensive, nourishing food; of exercise in the open air; of the practice of thorough mastication; of temperance in diet; and of abstinence from drugs and strong drink. But people — people in all income classes — are slow to act upon these counsels, and they destroy foolishly and recklessly their most valuable personal asset next to good character; viz., their health. Economic necessity excuses some, but only a very little, of this improvidence. The schools must teach their lesson more effectively and persistently; the department of health must carry on its propaganda under even better conditions and with greater resources; social workers and physicians must join hands even more effectively in their education of the public, upon which sound public sanitation and personal hygiene alike depend.

Disease has its social as well as its individual side, and the winning fight of society with one kind after another is one of the most satisfactory chapters in the history of civilization. The list of infectious diseases whose causes are known is being constantly lengthened, and each new discovery about the true nature of a pathogenic germ increases our power to guard against it. Eventually even the chronic diseases will, it is confidently hoped, yield to the persistent and well-planned campaign of science, as many of the infectious diseases have already yielded, and as spinal meningitis, for example, is at this moment before our very eyes reluctantly but surely giving ground.

Leprosy, the plague, cholera, yellow fever, typhus, and smallpox are names which recall to students of the history of civilization great scourges, substantially overcome by the brilliant discoveries of science and the application of the principles of preventive medicine. They are not necessarily overcome for all peoples or among us for all time. Disregard of suitable precautions would bring them back upon us, and some of them may be said to stand constantly at our doors, seeking entrance at the slightest relaxation of vigilance. The Bubonic plague, especially, may easily threaten any American community which does not exterminate its rats; and smallpox, though the Health Board reports but a single death from this cause in 1908, is apparently kept at bay only by the universal and continuous practice of vaccination.

Bubonic plague and Asiatic cholera are two of the so-called filth diseases which, for the moment at least, are of more direct concern to the Orient than to us. There are, however, two other diseases, quite as appropriately called filth diseases, which have still a very direct concern for us, though we are making great progress in controlling them. These are typhoid and dysentery, including with the latter summer complaint, cholera infantum, and similar diarrhœal diseases.[1] These diseases are everywhere recognized to be due to polluted water, infected milk, and dirty food. They are eliminated by purifying the water supply, building sewers, exterminating flies, abandoning wells in towns, and establishing severe and appropriate discipline wherever people are gathered, without previous experience and training, in camps or elsewhere with improvised sanitary arrangements.

In San Francisco, after the earthquake and fire, typhoid was remorselessly and successfully kept from the camps by the fact that the municipal government, recognizing its helplessness, turned to the army and

[1] Sternberg: Infection and Immunity.

asked that the military system of sanitation be established and maintained. Acting on the advice of a sanitary officer, Lieutenant-Colonel George H. Torney, who has recently been appointed surgeon-general of the army, the state and municipal health authorities, with the assistance of such sanitary officers of the army as could be spared to help them, maintained a rigorous discipline, as a result of which the health of the community as a whole, notwithstanding the destruction of the homes of the people — perhaps in part because of the destruction of those homes — actually improved. The abundance of plain and substantial food, and the outdoor life which prevailed in San Francisco in the three months following the disaster, may have been purchased at an unreasonably high price; but any community, if it chooses, may by less drastic and more appropriate means, without the previous trying experience of the destruction of property valued at between four and five hundred million dollars, derive the benefits that were then and there obtained. The rate at which any community is lowering its death-rate from typhoid and from intestinal diseases of infants, the two principal remaining filth diseases, is an approximate index of its civilization.

There are other diseases which quite as closely concern us as factors in the misery of our modern American communities. Of these, I may name together two very well-known diseases in order to contrast their character and effects. One of them — tuberculosis — has been slowly but surely disappearing, — too slowly and none too surely, but still on the whole, over a long period, and now fortunately again over a short period, actually diminishing. The other — pneumonia — has been as surely and not so slowly increasing. For two years pneumonia has stood at the head in the mortality tables of Greater New York, leading tuberculosis, heart disease, diseases of children, Bright's disease, and cancer, in the order named.

About tuberculosis there is much to say, but it is a familiar story and I shall not weary you by its repetition. Beseech and compel consumptives at large not to infect others; beseech and compel incipient consumptives to stop work for a time and go into a good sanatorium, or failing that, to get under the care of a competent physician; beseech and compel the municipal and state authorities to build more hospitals and sanatoria, — cheap, numerous, and well located for the early cases, substantial, comfortable, and within easy reach for the advanced cases; and help the families whose income is reduced. When consumptives and others follow this advice, we shall have done what the conditions call for to reduce the misery from this greatest of all scourges. For you will of course understand that the mortality alone is no test of the burdens imposed by a disease, but that we must also take into account other considerations.

These two prevalent diseases of the lungs, pneumonia and tuberculosis, present certain very striking contrasts:[1] the clinical course for pneumonia is, in a word, a sudden attack, a few days' serious illness, and a short convalescence. The clinical course for tuberculosis tells of an insidious and prolonged beginning, total disability, sometimes for many years, a long period of treatment, and care even after apparent cure. The average length of disabling sickness is four weeks or less in one case and a year or more in the other. The prognosis points, in the case of pneumonia, to probable recovery, the mortality being from ten per cent to thirty-eight per cent in general hospitals and less in private practice, although close medical attention and skilful nursing are so important in pneumonia, and the period for which they are required so brief, as to make this a disease especially suitable for hospital care. In the case of tuberculosis, the recovery of well-developed cases is rare, and the permanent arrest or cure of incipient cases, under the best care, takes place in from forty per cent to seventy-five per cent of the cases recorded.

Pneumonia is a disease of greatest importance in

[1] Arnold C. Klebs: *American Medicine*, December, 1903.

childhood and old age, only about a fourth of all cases falling between fifteen and fifty years of age, which may roughly be considered the active working period. Tuberculosis, on the other hand, is a disease of early adult life, nearly three-fourths of all deaths from it occurring between fifteen and fifty years of age. The increase which has taken place in the death-rate from pneumonia between 1890 and 1900 is chiefly under five years of age and above sixty-five. Between the ages five and sixty-five there has been a decrease. In the case of tuberculosis there has been a very noteworthy decrease, but this decrease has been chiefly under fifteen and over forty-five years of age, — greater in fact over sixty-five years of age; and there has been but a slight decrease, — in New York probably an actual increase, until last year, — in the deaths occurring between fifteen and forty-five years of age.

Diphtheria is one of the diseases that is losing ground. It is gratifying that the mortality which, previous to the use of anti-toxin, ran close to fifty per cent of all cases, has fallen to less than ten per cent, that its mortality when compared with population, *i.e.* its real death-rate, which, in the old city of New York, thirty-five years ago, was three per thousand — greater than that of tuberculosis to-day — has fallen until it is about one-sixth as great as at the high point of 1875. In view, however, of the progress made under favorable conditions, it is still a matter of great public concern that there were nearly two thousand deaths from the disease last year in Greater New York and more than sixteen thousand cases reported. The situation obviously calls for such wider application of existing knowledge as will relieve these sixteen thousand homes of the anxiety and burden which they were called upon to bear, and will spare these nearly two thousand homes the grief and loss which these preventable deaths occasion.

With pneumonia and diphtheria as brief, and therefore from the point of view of poverty less serious, diseases, we may group scarlet fever and measles. From the former there were in New York in 1908, 1333 deaths and 24,426 reported cases; from measles, which we are apt to think of as a comparatively harmless, childish complaint, there were nearly a thousand deaths, — more than from typhoid, though not so many as from suicide, more than half as many as from diphtheria, — but there were nearly forty thousand cases of measles in all, more than twice as many as of diphtheria, one-half more than of scarlet fever, and more than ten times the number of typhoid cases.

Measles, like scarlet fever, is a disease that has not been materially influenced by modern sanitary measures. Both in England and in this country the number of deaths has increased rather than diminished in some recent decades. More deaths occur in proportion to the population in cities than in the country, the greatest mortality occurring in infants less than one year old, and among young children.

"*Measles,*" reads a circular of the Glasgow Board of Health, "*is a dangerous disease, one of the most dangerous with which a child under five years of age can be attacked.* It is especially apt to be fatal to teething children. It tends to kill by producing inflammation of the lungs. It prepares the way for consumption. It tends to maim by producing inflammation of the eyes and ears.

"It is *a great mistake* to look upon measles as a trifling disease. The older a child is, the less likely is it to catch measles; and if it does, the less likely is it to die.

"If every child could be protected from measles until it had passed its fifth year, the mortality from measles would be enormously decreased. It is therefore a great mistake, because as a rule children sooner or later have measles, to say 'the sooner the better,' and to take no means to protect them from it — even deliberately to expose them to infection."

I have referred to the great scourges that have been eradicated, and to one that is, we hope, destined to be overcome by the vigorous campaign which is now in

OUT OF HEALTH

progress against it, and to the more acutely contagious diseases for which the instruments of destruction at least appear to have been forged. There are certain other diseases which to the medical profession as such appear less important, being somewhat in the nature of luxuries and not a very serious menace to life, but which from the point of view of the social welfare now really outrank the diseases which I have named and which appear higher up in the mortality tables. I refer to such disabling complaints as rheumatism, indigestion, influenza, colds, catarrh, bronchitis, and constipation; ailments which limit earning capacity, undermine vigor and energy, lower the physical tone, and prepare a way for more acute diseases which get the credit of complete disability and death. Defective eyesight and defective breathing apparatus should perhaps from our point of view be added to this category. I name them as altogether undervalued causes of misery. I challenge the medical schools and laboratories, the institutes of research and family physicians, as not having paid sufficient attention to these disabilities; but beyond this, and as a more fundamental diagnosis of the difficulty, I challenge society as having permitted here very grave maladjustments in not having appreciated the importance of ailments of this kind, and for this reason not having been willing to pay for the service of investigating their cause, their character, and their cure, or for the service of treating them in time.

I suppose that no medical authority would think of grouping together such diseases as I have named, as from the medical point of view they may have nothing in common; but for us they have this in common, that they increase to an enormous, though incalculable, extent the sum total of misery which men, women, and children have to bear; they prevent that enjoyment of the good things of life to which we are fully entitled by the extraordinary amount of hard work that we do, by the bounty of nature and the abundance of our inherited wealth. Let endowments for laboratory research be multiplied, and let those who are released from other duties and are fitted by inclination and training for the task bestir themselves to find out something directly applicable and useful about rheumatism and colds, — to take two of the most familiar examples of afflictions from which many suffer and about which, as nearly as I can make out, the medical profession at the moment confesses bankruptcy, — and we shall be even more ready than we now are to join in the pæan of praise which that profession so often exacts and, on the whole, so richly deserves.

It is true, as Dr. Osler has said, that "measure as we may the progress of the world — materially in the ad-

OUT OF HEALTH

vantages of steam, electricity, and the other mechanical appliances; sociologically, in the great improvement in the conditions of life; intellectually, in the diffusion of education; morally, in the possibility of higher standards of ethics — there is no one measure which can compare with the decrease of physical suffering in man, woman, and child when stricken by disease or accident." It is true, as he says, that this is one fact of supreme personal importance to every one of us, and it follows naturally that any halting in this process, any standing still while men, women, and children suffer by disease or accident, is equally a matter of supreme personal importance to every one of us.

While certain diseases, especially those which afflict young children, have rapidly diminished, there are others, like cancer, Bright's disease, diseases of the heart and circulatory organs, and insanity, that tend to increase. No doubt to some extent the increase in the one class of diseases is the inevitable consequence of the decrease in the other. If children do not die from neglect in infancy, from diphtheria, meningitis, measles, and scarlet fever in childhood, or from tuberculosis in early manhood, they are naturally kept alive to die of such diseases as more commonly afflict those who are past middle life. (Diagram 3.) We are not yet prepared to insist that all deaths by violence, as these germ

MISERY AND ITS CAUSES

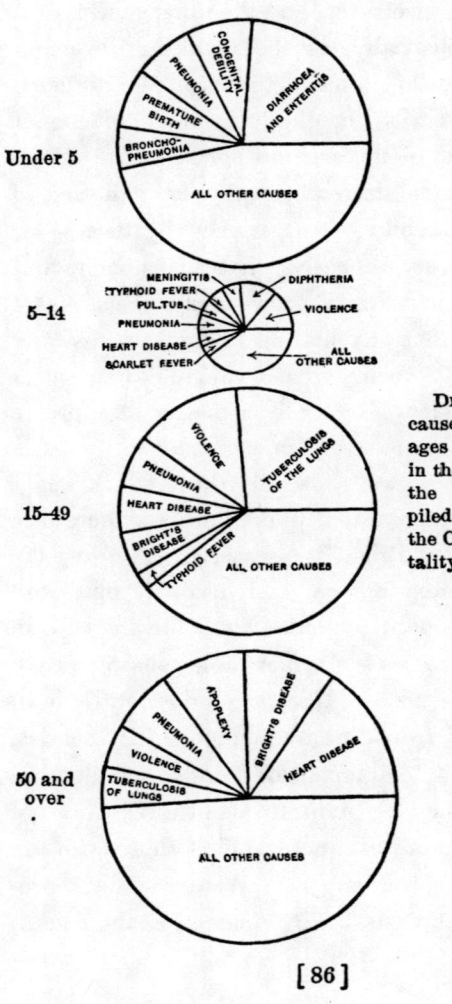

DIAGRAM 3. Principal causes of death at different ages (in four age-groups) in the registration area of the United States (compiled from the report of the Census Office on Mortality Statistics for 1906).

diseases have been called, shall cease, and that all shall live to die a genuinely natural death at an age expressed in three figures. Aside, however, from such changes in the mortality tables as are to be attributed to a mere postponement of death, brought about by the more rapid advances of preventive medicine in relation to diseases under middle age, there appear to be some causes at work which are distinctly favorable to the spread and increasing virulence of these diseases which are more frequently associated with more advanced age.

Scientists are keenly alive to the importance of discovering and counteracting these influences, and no doubt more intelligent effort is now being directed to the clinical and laboratory study of cancer, insanity, and the other increasing maladies, than to any other of the social maladjustments which fall within the range of our discussion.

No statement concerning the misery due to disease, however brief it must be, would be complete without a reference to the venereal diseases.

Fortunately, the existence of the American Society of Social and Moral Prophylaxis and its publications, which are readily obtainable, prevent the necessity of going in detail into a consideration of this painful subject. It is sufficient to point out that these diseases are probably more prevalent in large towns than any other, and that of the two most serious of these diseases, the milder and less dreaded is held to be responsible for a large part — probably twenty to thirty per cent — of congenital blindness, and for an even larger part — possibly forty-five per cent — of all sterile marriages.[1] Evidently here, rather than in deliberate restriction of the size of families, is the real race suicide. The other and more dreaded of the two principal venereal diseases, although less frequent, is for those whom it affects even more disastrous. No other disease is so susceptible of hereditary transmission, and no patient can with real safety ever be discharged as completely cured. Fortunately one-third of all syphilitic children die within six months, thus ending a miserable and harmful existence.

The case here is very analogous to that of tuberculosis. Certain clearly defined public policies are essential to social control of these two diseases. What is required first of all, as in the case of tuberculosis, is the more complete suppression of charlatanism. What is required next is popular education, especially of young people. We need, as Dr. Morrow has so clearly and convincingly pointed out, to break effectively the conspiracy of silence, and of that conspiracy, if he will allow me to say so, the name of the society which he has

[1] Morrow: Social Diseases and Marriage.

founded and to which I have referred — the American Society of Social and Moral Prophylaxis — appears to me an excellent illustration.

Certain specific measures may be advisable, such as are embodied in the law of Norway making the transmission of venereal disease a penal offence, or the requirement of a medical certificate as a condition of obtaining a marriage license, or the compulsory registration of this disease as contagious. But far more important than these is the popular education to which I have referred in another connection, education not in disease, but in health; not in the consequences of abuse and vicious indulgence, but in the joy and satisfaction of purity and health.

VII

Turning from considerations relating to the prevalence of specific diseases, there are some not unfamiliar facts which must be marshalled because they bear directly upon the amount and kind of misery from which we suffer. Diseases are not merely social, in that their prevalence and mortality depend upon infection, filth, public sanitation, hospital provision, and the state of medical science. They are also economic, and that in at least two ways: in relation to occupation, and in relation to income.

Many diseases are distinctly occupational; that is, they are far more prevalent in particular occupations because of conditions under which those occupations are carried on, conditions which as a rule the individual employee cannot control.[1] The caisson disease and the tunnel disease are illustrations which, although they affect comparatively few workmen, bring out very strikingly the extreme relation of health to occupation.

[1] Oliver: Dangerous Trades; and Diseases of Occupation. For a condensed discussion of the Hygiene of Occupation, see article by G. M. Price, in the Reference Handbook of Medical Sciences.

OUT OF HEALTH

High praise to the builder of tunnels who has at last bored beneath a mighty river without the loss of a single life. Dust-breathing trades, such as coal mining, stone-cutting, metal polishing and the textile industries, increase directly the diseases which affect the respiratory organs, and by so doing cause premature deaths, break up homes, multiply widows and orphans, increase the burdens and lessen the incomes of the families affected, and lower standards of living. There is a direct connection between the nervous strain of overwork and the speeding process and susceptibility to disease.[1]

I make all allowance for the personal factor. I realize that two men may stand side by side at the same bench, one of whom, because of a good heredity, exceptional resistance to infection, careful personal habits, and favorable outside home conditions, may go unscathed through experiences to which others of less than the average resisting power will speedily succumb. I do not undervalue personal abstinence from alcoholic beverages and from excesses of other kinds, but it is my idea that such a high standard of personal hygiene and self-restraint should naturally have the effect

[1] See papers by George M. Dock, M.D., and by Jane Addams and Alice Hamilton, M.D.; read in Section V of the International Congress on Tuberculosis, 1908.

of lengthening life and of giving a surplus physical enjoyment, and not merely at best enabling a man of robust constitution to withstand dangers by which society has surrounded him.

Certain occupations are extra hazardous, unnecessarily hazardous in any broad view of the matter, because of the danger of accidents, or poisons, or irregular hours, or excessive hours. Some occupations involve night work, dampness, exposure to heat, to injurious light, or to strain and unnatural positions. Some other occupations, not in themselves dangerous or injurious, become so merely because they are carried on in places where there is not sufficient light and adequate ventilation, or because they are in buildings not properly constructed for the purpose for which they are utilized. Work continued uninterruptedly may be far more injurious than the same work, under precisely the same conditions, with suitable pauses or change of position, relaxation, and bringing into play new muscles. Work which is suitable to some individuals may be entirely unsuited to others, even of the same race, nationality, age and size. Utterly stupid, gratuitously destructive of the health and comfort of employees, are the mechanical arrangements in many laundries, cigar factories, and other industries.

Much of the physical injury resulting from occupations would be avoided, even though precisely the same kind of work were done in the aggregate, if boys on going to work were sifted according to their capacity, and their occupations were chosen under professional advice, with reference to their particular physical constitution. There should be guidance in the selection of trades. Boys and girls choose their occupations largely by accident and fail to appreciate that certain trades should be followed only by the best physically endowed constitutions. If there were medical advice in the selection of trades, scrofulous individuals with a tuberculous family history would not embrace indoor, sedentary, inactive occupations, and those in which large quantities of dust must be inhaled. No child under eighteen years of age should be allowed to engage in any occupation except that of developing the physical and mental faculties. Women should not continue at work immediately before or after child-birth, or engage in occupations for which they are physically unfitted, or disregard their physiological need for complete suspension of labor at appropriate intervals.

Much of the misery traceable to occupations is due to the fact that homes are transformed into factories. We have long since reached the point at which all home manufacture must be looked upon as a maladjustment. Clothing should be manufactured in factories built for

MISERY AND ITS CAUSES

the purpose, equipped with proper machinery, manned by factory operatives, inspected by the appropriate state department, with ample ventilation, and if necessary, in order to secure these conditions, with a higher price to the consumer. What is true of clothing is true of such other manufacture as is still carried on in tenements.

VIII

The subject of industrial disease is still somewhat obscure — its twilight darkness not having been illuminated either by official investigation on a large scale, or by such continuous compilation of comparative statistics as would make such an inquiry feasible. A private life insurance company has done more than all our labor bureaus in this country to bring out the relations between occupations and disease. But there is another relation between industries and physical disability which is so obvious and direct that no dearth of official statistics, no silence of the public guardians of the interests of labor, can obscure it. I refer to death and injury by industrial accidents. Nor is the state in this matter entirely unmindful of its duty. We do now learn regularly, although probably not yet completely, from the State Labor Department about accidents in factories and quarries and tunnel construction, from the Public Service Commission about those which occur within their jurisdiction, and from the Interstate Commerce Commission about those which are reported as having occurred on railways. During the year 1908,

MISERY AND ITS CAUSES

251 persons were killed by accidents in factories, quarries, and tunnel construction in the state of New York; at least 1663 were permanently disabled; 1541 others seriously, probably permanently, injured; and 10,474 temporarily disabled. An even greater number, 444, were killed in accidents on the steam roads, subway and elevated roads and surface roads subject to the jurisdiction of the Public Service Commission for the first district, *i.e.* Greater New York; 2147 were seriously injured, and 32,469 other persons were injured in a less degree. (Diagram 4.) In the year ending June 30, 1908, 68,989 passengers and employees were injured, and 3764 were killed, on the railroads of the United States.

We have had no exhaustive study of accidents in this community. Fortunately, however, we have a very illuminating inquiry by Miss Crystal Eastman into the industrial accidents occurring in an industrial community in a neighboring state — an inquiry whose primary purpose was to ascertain precisely what fatalities and serious injuries among wage earners mean to the families of the victims.[1] This investigation extended to all the deaths recorded in the Coroner's office in the city of Pittsburg within a calendar year,

---

[1] *Charities and the Commons:* XXI, 561, 1143; and forthcoming volume published by Charities Publication Committee for the Russell Sage Foundation.

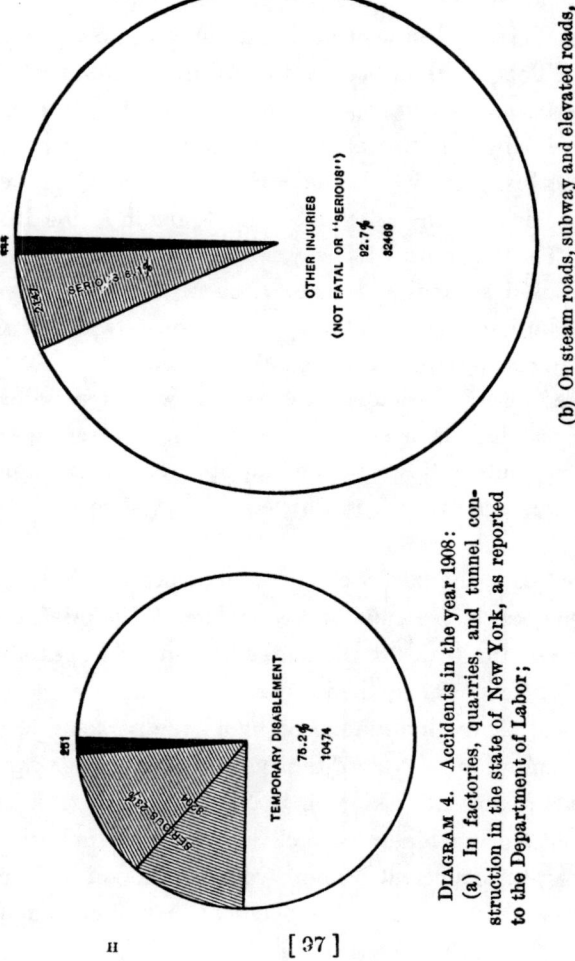

OUT OF HEALTH

DIAGRAM 4. Accidents in the year 1908: (a) In factories, quarries, and tunnel construction in the state of New York, as reported to the Department of Labor; (b) On steam roads, subway and elevated roads, and surface roads subject to the jurisdiction of the Public Service Commission for the First District (Greater New York).

and to all of the injuries within three months which were sufficiently serious to bring a patient into the hospital. There were in that year in Allegheny County 526 deaths from industrial accidents. This is half as many as were killed in the Slocum disaster and almost as many as lost their lives in the San Francisco earthquake. It is nearly as many as were burned to death in the Iroquois Theatre. Any railway wreck or other disaster that caused so many deaths at once, reckless as we are of human lives, would appear to be — what these deaths actually are — an appalling catastrophe. Two hundred and fifty-eight of the persons who were killed were married men supporting families, three were women contributing to the support of others, and 265 were single men from thirteen to sixty-five years of age.

The loss to the family of the wage earner who is killed is of two kinds, personal and economic. The grief, the loneliness, the wreck of plans, the blasting of hopes, the loss of the experience, the judgment, and the strength of the head of the household, make up the personal loss. These things are a part of that misery which I attribute to maladjustment, taking in this instance the form of unprotected machinery or reckless habits, or imperfect statutes, or inefficient administration either of government or of industry. This personal loss, though it is

OUT OF HEALTH

by far the most serious part of the injury, is incalculable. It is not so of the economic loss; that is largely calculable, and the calculation has been made.

The special object of the inquiry was to ascertain how this loss is distributed — whether it falls upon the families of the wage earners, or upon the employers, so that it may become in the first instance a burden upon the industry in which the wage earners are employed and thence be transferred, like any other cost of production, to the purchasers of commodities. The facts were obtainable in the case of 304 deaths of men who were contributing a part or the whole of the maintenance of the family. Two-thirds of them were married men. Of these 304 families, 88 received literally not one dollar of compensation from the employer; 93 families received not more than $100, a sum which would cover reasonable funeral expenses, but would not take the place of any share of the loss of income; 62 families received something over $100, but not more than $500; 61 families received more than $500 — most of them under $1000. In other words, 181 families — fifty-nine and one-half per cent — were left by employers to bear the entire income loss, and only 61 families, or twenty per cent, received in compensation for the death of a regular income provider more than a sum which would approximate

MISERY AND ITS CAUSES

one year's income of the lowest paid of the workers killed.

The earnings at the time of death were ascertained in the case of 193 of the married men. The wage loss to the families of these married men, based on their earnings at death and their expectation of life, according to the standard mortality tables, deducting $300 a year to cover the maintenance of the man who was killed and taking account only of what would have been available over and above this cost of his personal maintenance, would amount to $2,754,357. The total compensation made to these 193 families, including the sum for funeral expenses, was $72,039, or approximately two and one-half per cent of the actual loss.

Among the 288 persons whose injuries were less than fatal, and concerning whom the facts were ascertained, 164 were married men, nine were single men wholly supporting a family, eight were the chief support of the family, fifty more contributed regularly to the support of a family, and fifty-seven only were free from dependents. Miss Eastman justly points out, however, that in considering the hardships of these cases of injury we may not disregard the single men who have no one dependent upon them, as we may in cases of death; for the problem of existence for a single man disabled and

OUT OF HEALTH

deprived of income is serious enough even though there be no family to aid.

The proportion of loss borne by employers in these injury cases, in other words, by the industries in which the victims were engaged, does not differ greatly from that of the death cases. Fifty-six per cent of the married men received no compensation, 69 per cent of the single men contributing to the support of others received no compensation, and eighty per cent of the single men without dependents received no compensation; understanding, however, by compensation, compensation for their loss of income. Hospital charges were paid by the employer in eighty-four per cent of the injury cases, and frequently some outside medical expense was met, as for examination by a specialist or the purchase of an artificial limb. Nineteen of the 288 injured employees received full pay during the time they were disabled. Compensation in the remainder of the cases varied without any obvious relation to the need, length of disability, or other fixed principle; none of them received more than $1000, although six men were totally disabled for life. Of these six men thus totally disabled for the remainder of their natural lives, three received no compensation whatever aside from hospital care, one received $30, one $125, and one $365. Twenty-seven men were partially disabled for life, their earning power being reduced, on an average, nearly thirty per cent. Twelve of these men received no compensation; seven received $100 or less; and seven received more than $100, two of them over $500. Two hundred and twenty-nine who were temporarily disabled received an aggregate compensation of $6719, which is calculated to have been one-sixth of their pecuniary loss from accident. Some of those who were put down as partially disabled suffered from permanent injury which, while not totally disabling them, has seriously crippled their earning power or has caused a grave and painful affliction, which in some instances may have serious effects in after life. Three men for the loss of an eye received nothing; one man, $48; two men, $50 each; one, $75; one, $100; two, $150 each; and one, $200. For the loss of an arm two men received no compensation and one, $300. For the loss of a leg compensation runs from nothing to $225. Compensation, where any is indicated, included as a rule the cost of an artificial leg. There were ten men who lost two or more fingers: six received nothing; one, $15; two, $100; one for the loss of three fingers, $250. Compensation in the ten cases averaged $19 a finger.

Miss Eastman shows conclusively, with a wealth of illustrative detail and an incisive analysis of the objections to the whole plan by which the loss from accidents

OUT OF HEALTH

is distributed under our American laws and customs, that wages do not cover risks whatever the legal assumption to the contrary; that the doctrine of the assumption of risk and the responsibility of the fellow-servant are nothing less than a legal and judicial maladjustment.

It is a serious question whether the employers' liability laws in New York and in Pennsylvania are not really worse than no law at all. If the man who is injured had no legal claim whatever on his employer, but relied entirely upon his generosity, he would probably fare better than under existing conditions which give him a legal claim for damages in perhaps ten per cent of the cases of death or serious injury. The method of employers' liability is uneconomic and flagrantly unjust. To abolish it without substituting compensation on the English principle or insurance on the German principle would be an improvement, but it would not be just and it would not be wise. It is possible to work out a system which shall not be burdensome upon industry; which shall give prompt, sure, and reasonable compensation; which shall be free from all the absurdities, delays, and injustice of the existing system; which shall remove one of the chief causes of bitterness and class antagonism; and which, by operating to reduce the whole number of accidents, shall save us from a considerable part not only of the economic loss which we now distribute so unjustly and uneconomically, but also of that personal loss which is none the less real because we cannot express it in terms of money.

IX

The economic aspects of disease and physical disability are not exhausted by the consideration of occupational diseases, accidents, and other consequences of the conditions prevailing in certain industries. They take us into the home as well as into the factory. The amount of the family income and the standard of living which it permits have a direct relation to susceptibility to disease and the power of resistance. The decrease in disease is probably due quite as much to the general improvement in the standard of living, our greater wealth, the diffusion of knowledge, shorter hours of labor, the improvement of machinery, and such causes, as to advances in medical science and in preventive hygiene.

We cannot of course disentangle the effects of these two sets of influences, nor is there any advantage in doing so. I wish merely to emphasize the fact that many people are out of health and enduring the misery resulting therefrom as best they can merely because, from lack of income, they are living in overcrowded quarters, or taking in lodgers, or sending wife and

MISERY AND ITS CAUSES

children to work, or living without sufficient nourishment and recreation, and without prompt and efficient attention to their physical ailments.

Dr. Chapin's study of the standard of living in New York,[1] and Miss Byington's study of the Slavs in Homestead,[2] alike show that the true function of the lodger is that of a rent-paying necessity. Seventy per cent of the families in New York who reported lodgers were overcrowded. By every test that we may choose to apply, we find that families which are partially dependent upon the earnings of mother and children, and families which are dependent upon lodgers for a part of their income, have a lower standard, other things being equal, than those who live entirely upon the father's earnings. This is what one would naturally expect, but accurate observation and statistical analysis do not always, as so clearly in this instance, establish the expected.

The conditions which we find among the Slavs in Homestead are hard work, low wages, unsanitary homes, and an indifferent community. Taking lodgers is a common practice among them and it is not, as might be

[1] The Standard of Living among Workingmen's Families in New York City. Published by Charities Publication Committee for the Russell Sage Foundation.

[2] *Charities and the Commons*, XXI, 913; and forthcoming volume to be published by Charities Publication Committee for the Russell Sage Foundation.

OUT OF HEALTH

supposed, the giving of a home to a friend from the old country, nor letting an extra room which the family does not need for its own purposes. It is a deliberate business venture to increase the inadequate income from the man's earnings. It is not young couples without children, or elderly people whose children have left the parental roof, that take lodgers, but families with growing children; and it is to the health and morals, the comfort and discipline of these growing children that the practice is disastrous.

Overcrowding, and the resort to supplementary earnings by wife and children, obvious as are their disadvantages, are after all a means of escape from other hardships resulting from inadequate and irregular income. They are the price paid for food and shelter and the other necessities of life. Sometimes even these sacrifices are not sufficient to insure the elementary conditions of decent living. The Committee on the Standard of Living thought that it was a safe inference, from the data in their possession, that an income under $800, however earned, is not enough to permit the maintenance of a normal standard for a family of five persons in the city of New York. Nearly one-third of all the families studied by the Committee with incomes from $600 to $800 were underfed. The average expenditure for clothing was less than is necessary. The furnishings of apartments were inadequate. On an average less than ten dollars a year was spent on account of health; the dentist was completely ignored, and recreation and education, save as they are free, were reduced to the lowest terms. There was no provision for the future except at the sacrifice of necessary food or excessive overcrowding. Under such conditions infection gains a comparatively easy foothold, and the foundations are laid for an infinite variety of chronic ailments.

Misery springing from disease which is essentially economic will continue among us until workingmen are able to have a reasonable amount of light and air in their homes; to restrict the household to its natural members; to withhold children from gainful occupations until they have been prepared and have the necessary strength and maturity; until they are able to take a reasonable amount of recreation and to enjoy their holidays; to work without overwork; to consult a dentist or a physician, and if necessary a specialist, in time; in short, to have an income sufficient to provide for the essentials of rational living.

X

The subject to which I have invited your attention in this chapter is a depressing one. Out of Health is a most disagreeable theme. I have not been unaware of the incipient feelings of irritation and mental revolt which may have been aroused by thus dwelling upon this reverse side of our community life, when we might instead have been picturing the health and energy of human beings as they work and play. I hope that it is so; that in spite of these statistics of pathological conditions, these evidences of misery, we have been able to realize, as we should always realize, that this is but the reverse side.

Out of Health shall be replaced, as the theme of our closing paragraphs, with Out of Doors. I hold that the hope of the future — in this matter of health and vigor, in this matter of energy and activity, in this matter of life and enjoyment — lies primarily not in the test-tube of the laboratory, not in antitoxin or serum, not in quarantine or the killing of the mosquito or the rat, and not in the isolation of germs, but in rational living. These infectious diseases we must deal with, of course, and we must deal with them by appropriate means. Vermin must be exterminated, immunity must be effected, surgeons and physicians must have their appropriate instruments; but if our hope of health lay solely in these directions, it would be but a petty, artificial, mechanical, undesirable immunity that we should have attained.

We shall be a strong and healthy race because we have good red blood in our veins; because children are born into families that desire them and are ready to work for them and to make sacrifices for them and to teach them right methods of living; because we throw open our windows and go out into the fresh air, touching again, like Antæus of old, mother earth, from whom we draw our sustenance, not allowing our lives to be circumscribed by office walls or factory walls, or tenements or apartments, by subway trains and surface cars, by pavements and bill boards, by electric lights and all the fiendish noises of the towns. We cannot go backward, but by going forward we can bring back into our civilization some of the things which we have lost. We can organize fresh air and solitude and communion with nature; we can take stock of our industrial organization to find out whether it is conserving life or destroying life; and we can put an end to the maladjustments by which life is destroyed. We can save the babies from milk poisoning; we can save the children from the permanent disabilities resulting from neglect of their childish ailments; we can save the young girls from the dangers and the injuries attendant upon their employment in factories, department stores, or elsewhere; we can save the boys from loss of their manhood and fit them better by vocational training for a normal life; we can save the women from overwork, from work at all when they ought to be idle, and from injurious idleness when they ought to be occupied; we can save the men from industrial accidents, from death by tuberculosis and typhoid, and from that kind of shiftlessness and failure to provide for their families which is really due to malaria, indigestion, and other similar ailments; and we can save them, I believe, at last, from the terrible curse of alcoholism, which is half a disease and half a crime and altogether the greatest foe of health and vigor that we have.

We can save the babies, the boys and the girls, the men and women, from these things, but of course the "we" who can save them are but the "we" — men and women and children — who are to be saved. This is no paternalistic enterprise but, on the contrary, of the very essence of democracy. Democracy in the merely negative sense of kicking out the kings, the hereditary law makers, and the aristocracy, is after all a very paltry thing. The democracy to which we pledge our faith is the rule of the many with standards. This is the place for us to begin to erect our standards. The most elementary of all standards for which to secure recognition is the standard of health.

CHAPTER III

OUT OF WORK

I

INCOMES may be secured by gifts and inheritance, by fraud and violence, or by work for which compensation is received. The poor — like the well-to-do — furnish illustrations of all of these sources of income. Their income from gifts we call charity. Their income from violence and from fraud is comparatively negligible, for pocket picking and begging-letter writing and suchlike occupations, while disastrous enough to the character of those who resort to them, do not yield in the aggregate any such incomes as individuals may secure — with equally disastrous results to character — from wrecking railways and bribing courts and legislatures and municipal authorities, from mingling fraud with other ingredients in foods and medicines, and other such forms of violence and dishonesty as are mainly open only to those who have some income in advance. Those whom we call the poor probably derive on the whole a smaller proportion of their income from gifts and from preying upon society than do those who rank above them in the scale of incomes. Parasites, paupers, and criminals there are among them certainly. Begging and thieving are unfortunately among their sources of income. Those who strive successfully for the eradication of pauperism and of crime are the best friends of the poor; and I suspect that the wise and courageous teachers who strive for the eradication of similar weaknesses and defects among the rich, which take of course among them very different forms, are likewise the best friends of the rich. The little brothers of the rich and the big brothers of the poor are akin in spirit. They have somewhat the same discouragements, though the more powerful criminaloids may find ways not open to the poor criminal of striking back when the correcting rod smites their shoulders, and so perhaps the reformer who confines himself to pauperism and open crime has, on the whole, the easier time.

If I am right in my conviction that both gifts and thievings make up comparatively a negligible part of the income of the poor, and that, like farmers and skilled mechanics and the commercial classes and the professional classes, the poor live mainly on their earnings — then it becomes more important than workers among the poor have usually realized to consider the conditions under which those incomes are earned and the consequences of any interruption of those earnings, either for personal reasons, such as physical disability and bad habits, or for industrial reasons, such as contraction in the amount of employment available, changes

OUT OF WORK

in the location of industries, or the system of casual labor.

From the point of view of the charitable agencies, the importance of this subject is indicated by the fact that in two-thirds of the families who come under the care of the Charity Organization Society in industrially normal times one or more wage earners are unemployed at the time of their application for aid. This proportion, as one might have expected, was higher in 1907–1908, after the financial crisis, than in the preceding year, but the difference is not so great as might naturally have been expected. In 1906–1907, sixty-five per cent of the new families who applied for aid had some wage earner unemployed, either from personal disability or industrial conditions, and in 1907–1908 this was true of seventy-two per cent. This increase from sixty-five per cent to seventy-two per cent does not represent the full consequences among wage earners of the changed industrial conditions. No statistics of charitable societies will represent those consequences. It does bring out clearly, however, that even in prosperous times the distress which leads to application for charitable assistance is closely connected with the temporary cutting off of an income which is ordinarily, even if irregularly, earned.

Our records do not conclusively show the reasons for unemployment. Acute illness would naturally be ac-

MISERY AND ITS CAUSES

cepted as a sufficient explanation until you reflect that some of those who are acutely ill were unemployed before their illness and will be so again after their recovery. Intemperance would explain it, but then, unfortunately for that explanation, some of our intemperate men and women are not unemployed.

II

The besetting vices of those who from the two polar points of view discuss the unemployed are callousness and sentimentality. A thick-and-thin apologist of things as they are looks naturally on a fringe of unemployed workingmen just as he looks on a few unrented houses, a stock of unsold goods, or a surplus of uninvested capital. They are merely an incident, and an inevitable, normal, and desirable incident, of the labor market. If there were no unemployed, no new enterprises could be undertaken, labor organizations would become too powerful, wages would soar upwards, and the demands of workingmen for all kinds of reasonable and unreasonable conditions would have to be granted. A large surplus body of workers keeps those who are employed in a proper state of discipline, leaves the capitalist free to encourage any new undertaking which requires labor, confident that he can make his own terms with no nonsense about recognizing a union or agreeing on the terms of a collective bargain.

It is ordinarily assumed that the wage system, as it now prevails in mills, mines, building operations, stores and offices, and elsewhere throughout our industrial and commercial organization, does presuppose this constant presence of a fringe of the unemployed; that if in any industry for a period of years absolutely all workers were employed, so that employers could not resort to a threat, actual or implied, of replacing their present employees by others, the strength of the workers in the demand for higher wages and better terms would tend to become so great that the unregulated *laissez-faire* wage system would break down, and employers would take the initiative in asking for compulsory arbitration or the limitation of wages by statute, as they have so often done before when for exceptional reasons the supply of laborers was abnormally reduced.

The calm acceptance of a situation in which surrounding every industry there is an eager and perhaps half-famished ring of unemployed, whose presence undermines the natural strength of the employed workingmen, whose lower standards threaten their standard of living, whose necessities may be played off against the otherwise successful attempts of wage earners to increase their wages and improve their condition, is nothing else than callousness.

Apologists for existing conditions in this respect take their stand upon the eternal economic laws and rely upon the ultimate harmony between the self-interest of the individual and the broad interests of society. I also believe in that harmony of interests, and in the justice of the fundamental economic principles upon which our industry and commerce are founded. But I see in many places maladjustments for which our greed and ignorance, our short-sighted policies, and our inefficient social control are responsible, which disturb those harmonies and pervert those laws.

The unemployed are made up of an extraordinary combination of the results of such maladjustments. Some of these we can, if we will, readjust radically and at once. Others we can for the time being only bear with patience, as penalties for our own mistakes, or as voluntarily assumed burdens originating in the mistakes of others and transferred to us. But the first thing of all is for us to see clearly that no rational system of industry — no such system as is consistent with our American laws and traditions and public standards — requires or contemplates this unemployed fringe.

In any community there are growing into maturity and earning capacity every year a host of boys eager to take the place of the generation which is passing into industrial retirement. This is the natural, inevitable, essential fringe, which corresponds under normal conditions to the uninvested capital and the unsold stocks of goods. When, in addition to these, there are injected into the industrial system large masses of laborers from foreign lands, who come not in a slow and moderate international adjustment of surplus labor, but in millions, because of religious persecution elsewhere, because of misrule, because of political revolution, because of the collapse of the economic system of an entire nation, because of a widespread network of solicitation by agents of transportation companies, because of a demand not for labor, but for cheap labor, then it is evident that there is a maladjustment — a violent and unnatural disturbance of the equilibrium which the economic laws tend to establish. This is, however, one maladjustment which I had in mind in suggesting that it may be better to endure it with all its burdens and with all the actual injustice which it inflicts on American workingmen. Possibly we may be nearing the end of that great world movement of populations toward us, which, beginning in the British Islands and Scandinavia, has swept down through Germany to Italy and southeastern Europe, emptying one area after another of its surplus population. Possibly Africa, South America, and Siberia, rather than the United States, will absorb the greater part of what remains, so that the menace of unrestricted immigration will of itself pass away through the reëstablishment of a more stable equilibrium and the substitution of more virgin lands than ours in whatever further readjustment of population may still need to take place. A more strict regulation of immigration than has prevailed would have been advisable. We have missed an opportunity for selection such as has never before been presented, and for an improvement of the stock that might have been secured. We have striven — not very successfully — to keep out the enfeebled and diseased, the insane, the pauper, and the criminal, and we have admitted without hindrance a very large number who have made life harder for wage earners already here, and have swollen the number of the unemployed; but looking ahead, the policy of restriction appears to me likely to be of diminishing importance. It has never been popular, because of its obvious conflict with our ideal of America as the asylum of the oppressed. Very well, let us cherish the ideal, but let us frankly recognize what it costs, and one of those costs is certainly the very serious complication of our problem of the unemployed.

III

The effect of immigration is not the only maladjustment which that problem presents. Disabling uncompensated accidents and industrial diseases, which I have discussed in another connection, are another. Accidents to tramps on unpoliced railways is another. Unemployed they usually are of course at the time of injury; but unemployed they remain permanently, partly on account of the injury; and of these there are some thousands chronically among the unemployed.

Another cause of maladjustment arises from the displacement of labor by new machinery or new industrial processes. Some drivers on the old horse-cars, of which we cherish a few relics in New York, became motormen, and some of the engineers and firemen on the elevated steam railways showed sufficient adaptability to fit into the electric service; but others were crowded out by the substitution of electricity for animal and steam power and contribute to the number of the unemployed. Compositors in printing-offices succeeded, because of their unions, in controlling to some extent the conditions under which type-setting machines could be introduced, and the financial resources of the typographical unions have been sufficient to care for some of those who were unable to adjust themselves to machine composition. But, especially in the country offices and in open shops, the old time tramp printer, intemperate in habits, an easy victim to tuberculosis and other diseases, furnishes a typical illustration of the stranded worker, who is at first irregularly, then frequently, and then chronically, and then entirely, unemployed.

It is notorious that the insatiable factory wears out its workers with great rapidity. As it scraps machinery so it scraps human beings. The young, the vigorous, the adaptable, the supple of limb, the alert of mind, are in demand. In business and in the professions maturity of judgment and ripened experience offset, to some extent, the disadvantages of old age; but in the factory and on the railway, with spade and pick, at the spindle, at the steel converters, there are no offsets. Middle age is old age, and the worn-out worker, if he has no children and if he has no savings, becomes an item in the aggregate of the unemployed. The veteran of industry who is crowded out by changes in processes and the use of new machinery is obviously an instance of maladjustment. The majority are not thus crowded out; the majority are able to turn themselves to new methods. The reason why a certain proportion — constituting a large number absolutely when compared with the unemployed, although a small number relatively when compared with those who remain at work — are unable to make the new adjustment is that their education was originally incomplete. They have had no general training back of their immediate trade such as ought to be provided by the public educational system for all boys before they enter upon their particular calling. Assuming health and a fair average degree of general efficiency, men ought to be able to change from a more primitive to a more complex occupation without great difficulty. Already the change is far easier than it used to be. The gulf separating one trade from another is not so wide as the present traditions of employers and the policies of trade unions presuppose.

I am indebted to Herbert S. Brown for an admirable statement of the possibility of much freer movement from one occupation to another than is actually taking place. Mr. Brown says: —

The natural limits to occupational mobility are, I believe, vastly less confining than those narrow bounds set down by custom, by habit, by employers, and by trade unions. The long apprenticeships demanded in some trades are sheer humbug, designed to keep down the total of workmen available in the craft. That the apprentice appears slow means almost always that he is not given the chance to learn —

OUT OF WORK

assuming, of course, reasonable energy and natural fitness for the work.

Back of each skilled trade and occupation lies primarily nothing more mysterious than a certain deftness of hand, accuracy of eye, coördination of muscles, sense of rhythm, commercial instinct, or whatever else it may be, essential to the profitable prosecution of that occupation. Many a one of such human qualities will open the way to success in more than one trade, — the more general of them to a large number of trades. For example, the man who has the "mechanical instinct," and has had sufficient training in any one of the score or more trades to have acquired accurate and quick coördination of brain and muscle, can and frequently does pass freely from one trade to another, with no greater handicap than the few weeks' or months' delay requisite to learn the special processes of the new trade and to bring his speed up to that of the man whose longer experience has made the work practically automatic. And the lower the grade of skill required, the easier to make transitions. It is unreasonable to expect, and secure, of the men who carry on the difficult work of the world, the astonishing mobility which history relates of Julius Cæsar, or Goethe, or the ex-plumber Croker, with many another immortal not yet dead enough to mention by name, and then deny to the deft fingers that roll cigarettes in hopeless competition with automatic machinery the chance at a dozen other occupations unknown to them but known to us where the deft finger is a valuable asset.

I believe that it is possible to weave through the maze of endlessly divided and subdivided craft and occupation a comparatively simple classification based on the underlying essential, human qualification, rather than on a technical knowledge of trade peculiarity. I believe it would be possible to pass men properly qualified, under such a classification, from one occupation to others closely allied with comparative ease. And I believe that the encouragement of such interoccupational mobility would be of very great benefit to the community. It is part of my creed in life that every man has a place, perhaps a dozen places, into which, when at last found, he will fit with definite profit to himself and every one else concerned. I believe that "congested" population means congested wealth, and that, with proper mobility facilitated, the tangle will resolve itself, so that ultimately we may be able to say, the more people the more prosperity.

If this view is sound, as I believe it to be, it follows that the changes within any particular trade, resulting merely from the invention of a new tool, a new machine, new and more effective ways of making combinations, ought to be possible for almost any competent workingman, and that in the comparatively few instances where new machines or new processes really mean revolution, changing the character of a trade, there should open up a comparatively easy change to another trade which in the demands that it makes upon workers is on the level with that of the machine or process which has been abandoned.

OUT OF WORK

The maladjustment, as you will see, is in part in the educational system, but in a larger part even more nearly at hand awaiting only an awakening to possible changes of occupation which unadjusted individuals might even now make without serious difficulty.

The accession to the numbers of the unemployed caused by old age, especially by old age at what ought to be the full maturity of middle age, presents a more difficult problem. The very changes from one trade to another, of which I have just been speaking, presuppose the adaptability, the suppleness, the alertness of youth, the very qualities the lack of which has caused these particular individuals to be displaced. The remedy, therefore, lies in the lengthening of the effective working period of human life — a slower and more fundamental change, but this also is taking place. The great advances in preventive medicine, as we have already seen, are overcoming the diseases incident to childhood and youth, and the effect of this will certainly be the strengthening of the period of middle life, the carrying forward into manhood of the qualities which put a premium upon youth.

We shall probably not slacken the pace of the wheels of industry, but we may get the stiffness out of the joints of the middle-aged man. We shall not create conditions which will lessen the advantage of the capacity for turning from one occupation to another slightly different, but we may increase the number of people who have this capacity and lengthen the period during which this ability is maintained. We may not be able to use less efficient workers, but we may increase the occupational mobility of those who are efficient, and the ease with which they change from one trade to another allied to it. We may recognize that individuals suffer and that the industries of the nation as a whole suffer from the lack of this occupational mobility and from the shortness of the working period.

The individual employer, it is true, may be able to keep his working force efficient though the units in it change rapidly. He scraps his machinery at his own expense, but heretofore he has been allowed to scrap his labor at the expense of the families of the laborer and the charities of the community. It has been in this respect a callous age, that it has not recognized that such rapid wearing out of human lives as does take place should be a burden upon the industry in which it occurs rather than upon charity or upon wives and children. Compensation for accidents and for occupational diseases, and retiring pensions in old age, are to be the order of the day.

As a matter of fact, frequent changes are a disadvantage to employers also, though not so great as the disadvantages to the community. Already a steel manufacturer has arisen to declare that strictly on business grounds he cannot afford to permit conditions that use up his workingmen, and a large employer of railway labor in the northwest is emphatic in his opinion that his primary concern is to give even to common laborers engaged in construction such treatment that they will desire to remain or to return season after season in preference to looking for work elsewhere. In other words, even in common labor permanency of tenure is seen to be an advantage to the individual employer as it undeniably is to the community as a whole.

Casual labor is the greatest of all maladjustments. The man who changes constantly from job to job, with periods of idleness between, comes to every job demoralized, unskilled, unsteady, and unfit. But casual labor, as matters now stand, is still demanded in some industries. It is a convenience to the employer, and that from the broader point of view it is an economic and a social maladjustment does not occur to him, or if it does, he declines to see why the burden of bringing about a readjustment should fall upon him. It is the employer therefore who in the first instance needs readjustment.

When the Charity Organization Society in the

neighboring town of Bayonne a few years ago went to the managers of the coal yards, and asked that instead of keeping twice the number of men actually needed on an average through the year in the constant expectation of occasional work they should give notice definitely that they would give preference to married heads of families, and would, to the utmost of their ability, distribute their work in such a way that these permanent resident heads of families should be able to do it; and when the managers of the coal yards gave a favorable response to this suggestion and made it clear to a lot of men whom they had irregularly employed as casual laborers that there would be no work at all for them and that it would be well for them immediately to look elsewhere, there was, although on a small scale, a prophetic advance in the direction of a very essential readjustment.

Seasonal trades have some of the demoralizing influences of casual labor, periods of feverish overwork alternating with periods of idleness. The reports made to the Department of Labor by representative trade unions in the state of New York show the fluctuations in employment among the workingmen who are on the whole most fortunately situated. The percentage of members unemployed for all reasons at the end of the month varies in normal years from six or

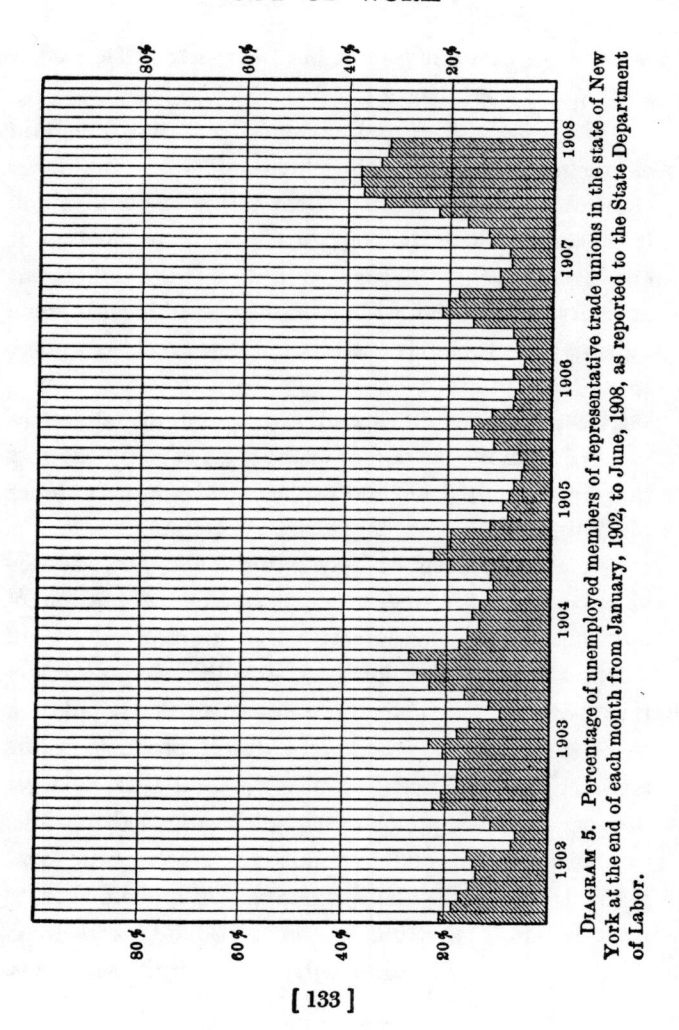

OUT OF WORK

DIAGRAM 5. Percentage of unemployed members of representative trade unions in the state of New York at the end of each month from January, 1902, to June, 1908, as reported to the State Department of Labor.

seven in August and September to twenty in December and January. (Diagram 5.)

This system of casual, intermittent, and uncertain employment is one with which not even the large charitable societies are fit to deal. It is one with which it is very difficult for organized labor to deal; but employers, acting through well-directed employment agencies, could deal with it if they would, with some advantage to themselves and with very great advantage to the community.

The growth of cities and towns and the abandonment of farm life is another of the revolutionary changes that have resulted in the misplacing of a large number of individuals. The migration of population to the urban centres is an entirely natural and not undesirable change. On the whole, a smaller proportion of our population will hereafter live upon the land, at least as agricultural laborers, for the simple reason that it requires a smaller proportion of the population to produce our food and agricultural products. The commodities which we require demand that a larger proportion of the population shall be engaged in trade, in transportation, and in industry. I have little sympathy with the popular watchword "Landless men to manless land," for the reason that landless men on manless land will ordinarily mean fruitless farms.

OUT OF WORK

But I have a keen sympathy for policies that will restrict congestion and enlarge the areas in which these urban populations may live. I have great sympathy with the establishment of colonies of people who really have the qualities which will enable them to succeed in agricultural pursuits. I have great sympathy for picking out the exceptional man and family that naturally belongs on the farm because of previous training or experience or inheritance or personal adaptability, and I have still greater sympathy for plans that will enable those who are actually on farms to become so prosperous by more scientific agriculture, by improved business organization, by coöperative methods and otherwise, that they can profitably remain there. The maladjustment here lies not in the mere relative increase in urban population, but in the mistakes by which individuals who ought to remain on farms get into the towns, either through misunderstanding and ignorance, or through the absence of that degree of success and of enjoyment which country life might easily afford.

IV

Such, then, are some of the maladjustments which are responsible for the lack of income from unemployment, irregular employment, and unemployability, immigration, uncompensated accidents, industrial changes, the displacement of workers prematurely disabled by old age, the lack of a reasonable degree of occupational mobility, and the growth of urban population. In our generation we have seen these influences acting on an unprecedented scale, in every conceivable combination, and with disastrous consequences to large numbers of workingmen and their families. When to these economic changes we add the complications arising from disease, from feeble wills and deficient original physical and mental endowment, or inadequate moral training and deficient or inappropriate intellectual and manual training, we begin to find an explanation of bread lines, homeless men, and other apparently able-bodied unemployed.

I would not minimize the influences of those financial and industrial crises, as a result of which mills close down, railways reduce their tonnage, builders cease their operations, and thousands of people who are

OUT OF WORK

ordinarily continuously employed are thrown out of work. Whether railways and mills need begin their policy of retrenchment, made necessary by a reduction of business, by the wholesale discharge of large numbers of laborers, whose incomes are at best barely enough to support their families and to maintain a desirable standard of living, is a question which only the directors and stockholders of the companies can ultimately decide. An official of one of the large railway systems has recently expressed to me his conviction that this policy, so contrary to that which is followed even in the clerical staff of the railway companies, is both cruel and unjust. On a week's notice, or on no notice, out they go, without insurance benefits, without personal consideration, without the possibility of finding other work, for the reason that the depression which has led to their discharge is likely to affect temporarily all the other occupations to which they would naturally turn. This contingency, like old age and sickness, is one for which I believe provision might be made by some insurance plan, though it is no doubt more difficult to arrange its details.

It is very greatly to the credit of workingmen and an evidence of their strength that, for the most part, even during the past two years of trial and strain, those who are ordinarily employed have been able to take care of themselves, — not without hardship, not without reducing their savings, not without lowering their standards of living, not without changing their occupations, not without moving to other places, and, in the case of aliens, not without returning in large numbers to their homes abroad; but to a very limited extent indeed have the able-bodied men who are ordinarily regularly employed appeared in the bread lines or in the municipal lodging-house or at the offices of charitable societies. They have come in limited numbers, in some cities more than in others, but for the most part they have relied upon themselves and upon such mutual assistance by relatives and friends and unions as makes no public show.

A period of widespread and general unemployment does increase the burdens of charitable agencies, because to some extent it closes resources which are ordinarily open to the sick and disabled, to widows and orphans, and to those who are otherwise taxed beyond their reasonable strength. The helpless cannot get the help from their immediate friends which they ordinarily get, and therefore they turn to the societies. The increased burden on the charitable agencies is not due to any great extent directly to applications for assistance from the families of genuinely able-bodied men.

V

I have recently had the honor of submitting to the Russell Sage Foundation a report on the desirability of establishing an employment bureau in the city of New York.[1] The inquiry which led to this report was instigated by a suggestion that such a bureau should be established upon a business basis, with an ample working capital, subscribed not primarily in the expectation of profit, but from a public-spirited desire to be of actual assistance to the unemployed, and in the belief that that assistance could be given more effectively and with greater assurance of permanency if employers at least were required to pay for the services which the bureau could render. The investigation disclosed that a large proportion of existing commercial employment agencies are conducted not upon a legitimate business basis, but upon an exploiting, extortionate, semi-fraudulent basis; that, in this country, free public employment bureaus have not

[1] Published by Charities Publication Committee for the Russell Sage Foundation.

been conspicuously successful, but on the contrary have been as a rule perfunctory, political, and of very limited usefulness; that the want advertisements, while acting as an intermediary with fair success in certain occupations, are in many instances vague and misleading, and that the degree of their usefulness is by no means indicated by the space which they occupy on the padded page of many newspapers; that trade unions, the ordinary means of communication between employers and employees in the trades which are most completely organized, have thus far not developed in most occupations a systematic and effective mechanism for this purpose, and that such mechanism as they have is not adapted to bring about the distribution of surplus labor to other communities or from one occupation to another.

Since existing commercial agencies, free public employment bureaus, want advertisements, and the unions are found not to be meeting the need, there remains the method of throwing upon individual workingmen the responsibility of going about from place to place to make personal application for work. This is the time-honored method much in favor with those who look with misgiving upon any relief policies or even upon changes in business methods which seem likely to undermine the feeling of personal responsibility; but it is an expensive, time-consuming, physically laborious, and mentally depressing process.

The conclusion which I have reached is that there is at present a maladjustment between work and workers, both within our own community and as between communities, and that there is a loss of time and serious hardship involved in the search for labor which might be obviated by the creation of an employment exchange, or work market, well organized and managed, with facilities that would enable it to bring about a quick adjustment between those who are unemployed and work that they might be capable of doing, whether in their own immediate neighborhood or at a distance. Such a bureau can, to some extent, deal with congestion of population on the only natural basis — that of finding employment in less congested neighborhoods; it can, to some extent, deal with the evil of casual labor by moving men quickly without the waste of time and the demoralization incident to intermittent periods of idleness; it can, to some extent, deal with the evil of misplaced labor, becoming vocational in the sense of studying carefully its candidates for employment with a view to securing the kind of work which they can do best; it can deal with the abuses of exploiting commercial agencies, bringing to bear upon them a competition like that which the

MISERY AND ITS CAUSES

Provident Loan Society brought to bear upon the old, unregulated pawn shops, and which the model tenements have brought upon unsanitary and indecent tenements.

The employment bureau is not a complete solution of the problem of the unemployed, but if rightly managed it would in the long run help materially in the solution of the problem of our ignorance in regard to the real extent and character of the problem of the unemployed. It would help individuals at any rate, and whether it were to succeed or fail as a business enterprise it would help us to understand what needs to be done. In so far as the unemployed are so because of sheer industrial contraction, because there is no work anywhere to be had, the employment bureau would not solve it. For that, prosperity is the only solution. In so far as the unemployed are utterly incapable and unfit to be employed, the bureau is no solution. For that, education is the only solution. In so far, however, as the surplus labor in one place is counterbalanced by insufficiency in another, and in so far as the unemployed are unable to find opportunities which really exist even in their own neighborhood, the employment bureau would help to meet the difficulty; in so far as it is an instance of maladjustment between work and workers it could help to effect an adjustment. To those who will undertake to try out this experiment there will come what appears to me to be one of the greatest opportunities that has yet been presented in connection with the making of a broad, constructive social programme.

VI

Sentimentality, the second of the two besetting weaknesses of many of those who begin to talk or write about the unemployed, has a curiously paralyzing effect upon the intellect, quite as disastrous as that paralysis of the sympathy which we call callousness. There are people who could not apparently, to save their lives, at least not to save their reputations, make a perfectly straight unvarnished statement even about such facts as actually are or certainly ought to be in their possession. The number of the unemployed known to them, the number who come to them for help, the number whom they place in positions, the number among these who succeed, the effect of cold weather, the effect of spring weather, — on these and on many other very interesting and important points they throw out an inky cloud of reckless and utterly misleading reports and interviews and epistles, which are gravely accepted in newspaper offices and pulpits as if they had some demonstrable reference to facts. An unemployed man becomes in their hands a mystery, such stuff as dreams are made of — pipe dreams.

OUT OF WORK

He is a thing apart, not to be treated like other mortals but cherished, coddled, lamented when he disappears, magnified by hocus-pocus statistics when he consents to materialize, but whisked away into the never-neverland when you approach too near. Ninety-nine and a half per cent of him does well on farms,[1] but when a letter is received offering twenty-five dollars a month and board for a man who is a fast milker, it is a subject for high merriment.[2] Why should one of the charmed circle of the unemployed be expected to become a fast milker? Ridiculous. And twenty-five dollars a month — laughter — and board — great laughter. Lay it on the table of course. The impudence of the farmer who expects any such return as that for his absurd wages and his board forsooth!

The unemployed as a stock in trade, as a stage property, so to speak, must have these elements of mystery, these sacrosanct features. But as human beings, with the ordinary faults and virtues, why should they not be brought to the same tests to which the employed have to submit as a matter of course? Where they live, what they can do, their physical condition, and their personal reputation are matters of

---

[1] See, for example, the *New York Herald* for February 14, 1909.
[2] Current newspaper report of a meeting of the unemployed in Chicago.

MISERY AND ITS CAUSES

legitimate interest to those who are asked to provide employment, or to initiate public policies in their behalf. When we cease to take seriously the silly sentimental generalizations about the unemployed, and think instead of individual men out of work, we shall find, I think, a real need for at least three things: a compulsory colony for vagrants; a voluntary colony for those who need and are willing to accept instruction and discipline without compulsion; and an employment exchange, or work market, with distinct departments for the several kinds of labor. I deprecate callousness and I deprecate sentimentality, but I urge upon thinking and public-spirited citizens very serious and persistent attention to these real needs.

CHAPTER IV

OUT OF FRIENDS

I

LET us begin our study of friendlessness with the ash barrel foundling. What more wretched object of pity could I conjure before your imagination than the infant abandoned in the hour of its birth, unacknowledged, unsheltered, and unnamed; pathetic token of misery, unconscious of its shame, exposed to the buffetings of chance, the child of ignorance and sin, and yet a human child?

Fielding, in introducing his foundling "Tom Jones," puts into the mouth of the worthy housekeeper words which exquisitely express a certain conventional attitude towards these "misbegotten wretches, whom," she says, "I don't look upon as my fellow-creatures. If I might be so bold, I would have it put in a basket and sent out and laid at the church warden's door. It is a good night, only a little rainy and windy, and if it was well wrapped up and put in a warm basket, it's two to one that it lives till it is found in the morning. But if it shouldn't, we have discharged our duty in taking proper care of it, and it is, perhaps, better for such creatures to die in a state of innocence than to grow up and imitate their mothers; for nothing better can be expected of them."

Unfortunately for her respectable views, but fortunately for Tom Jones, the master of the house got one of his fingers in the baby's hand, "which, by its gentle pressure, seeming to implore his assistance, had certainly outpleaded the eloquence of Mrs. Deborah had it been ten times greater than it was;" and such was her discernment and the respect in which she held the master, that her scruples gave way to his commands and she finally took the child, we are told, under her arms, without any apparent disgust at the illegality of its birth and, declaring it was a sweet little infant, walked off with it to her own chamber.

On reflection, I shall not dwell upon the friendlessness of any infant child that is allowed to live. Unfortunately, for the great majority of such foundling children, we still pursue the strictly correct, but for the child fatal, policy recommended by Mrs. Deborah Wilkins. We put them not at the church warden's door, but in a hospital, where they thrive about equally well, although it has been shown by actual experience in New York City that by another method almost as good a chance of life can be given these motherless infants who become public charges as the average

OUT OF FRIENDS

child has under normal conditions in a healthy community.

Private institutions under religious auspices seek to take the place of parents who feel constrained to abandon their infants, and in one way or another the period of friendlessness in the case of physically normal infants generally comes speedily to an end. Grim Death himself is the kind friend who often adopts the child, but if he can be kept at a distance human friends are always ready to perform, even for these misbegotten children, some such service as the Squire performed for Tom Jones.

Much the same thing is true of older children whom death or abandonment leaves friendless at a tender age. For these children also, if they are really without friends and relatives, foster homes are waiting. For a few misfits there may remain a long period of maladjustment during which the institution or the boarding home may be essential, but, paradoxical as it may seem, the reason for the large institutional population of children is precisely that they are not out of friends, that a surviving parent or grandparents, or aunts or uncles, or brothers or sisters — some near of kin — desire to retain their hold upon the child, usually a very natural and proper desire, one which must be taken into account and one which is often the decisive and controlling factor in the situation. Charitable societies, officers and teachers in institutions for children, as well as the relatives, and other private citizens if you give them a chance, are friends of these children, and they are by no means to be described as out of friends. For the real orphans who have none to claim them family homes are to be found, so that the friendlessness of the orphan child, like the friendlessness of the foundling, is but a brief and passing period and need not detain us.

II

We come next to the stranger, the grown boy and girl, the young man and woman, or the adult of mature years, who comes to the city without friends. For the best and strongest among them it is a time of peril and trial; for the weak and ignorant to be out of friends is disaster.

The young man who moves to a new community without introductions and connections which will bring him quickly into new social relations discards a certain part of his working capital. It is true that he may be well advised in doing so. A business or professional opening or a call for special service of a kind that he can render may be, under given circumstances, of more importance than friends. But if he comes as a homeless tramp, there is no such offset; and if the disability of sickness or of failure in business overtakes even the worker where there are no friends; and especially if, by any act of folly or from the exceptional necessity which does sometimes arise, the victim of such misfortune in a strange community has

MISERY AND ITS CAUSES

put it out of his power to return to his home or to call upon his earlier friends, — then the natural consequences of his sickness, or his lack of work, or any other such misfortune as may come upon him, are multiplied beyond calculation.

The Greeks, in their comparatively simple civilization, without automobiles or ocean liners, without steam or electricity, without congestion of cities or depopulation of farms, without overwork or unemployment, without sanitation or insanitation — the Greeks, in their simplicity, had one word for friend and guest, for stranger and barbarian. This was not because of the poverty of their language. It was because to them, under the conditions in which they lived, the stranger was the guest, the friend, the royal claimant to all the privileges of hospitality, the foe and stranger on the battlefield, but the guest-friend this side the threshold.

Increasing density and mobility of population have changed all that. The assize of Clarendon over seven centuries ago in England, in order to check crime and vagrancy, in the interests of peace and security, provided that no stranger should remain in any place except in a borough, that even there he must remain not more than one night unless sureties were given for his good behavior, and that a list of the names

OUT OF FRIENDS

of these strangers must be handed to the magistrate. After seven centuries of such legislation, now relaxing a little and now tightening again, the Royal Poor Law Commission, which has just submitted its report, takes the liberal position that settlement shall be gained in one year instead of three, and that the county be adopted as the normal administrative area instead of the parish, as in earlier days, or the union of parishes which is now the unit of poor law administration, and proposes to deal comprehensively, by labor colonies and otherwise, with the vagrant.

In this country the appellation "stranger" has, on the whole, had a significance very like that given to it by the Greeks. To be hailed as "stranger," especially in the south and west, is to be put upon a footing of just so much intimacy and good-fellowship as subsequent acquaintance may show that you are entitled to. We mix so easily, and move so rapidly, and strike roots in a new ground so naturally, and tear them up again on such slight provocation, that settlement and legal residence have, for the most part, only an arbitrary, technical significance. And yet with us also home has a deep and tender meaning. The institution of "home week" in the older New England states brings a response. Family reunions are the chief attraction of the Christmas and Thanksgiving holidays, and friend-

MISERY AND ITS CAUSES

ship is still — rather than hatred, or patriotism, or love itself — the master passion. At home and among friends every man is a more complete man, with a better chance both to earn and to live.

III

Friendship is too sacred and too great a theme to be treated here, as it were parenthetically, but it is the true contrasting background of our inquiry. Friendlessness, as nothing else in the last analysis, is misery. One is not reduced to this condition merely by geographical distance, and very seldom indeed merely by the passing of time. The old outlive particular friends, but they do not normally from the passing years alone become friendless. The farmer-boy moves into the town, but normally the post-office and the railway and the recurring holidays are gracious ministers to keep him in touch with his friends, and normally he finds in his own experience that the world is very small indeed.

The church exists primarily to prevent that friendlessness which tends to become misery and disaster. The church of every creed proclaims one common Father and the brotherhood of man; the church seeks out the stranger to give him friends, to make certain demands upon him, and to respond to those demands is forthwith to cease to be friendless and alone. I have understood the Commissioner of Public Charities to say that no man comes to the Municipal Lodging House or to the Bowery bread line through the route of regular attendance at church and Sunday-school. I have not examined the statistics upon which he bases this conclusion, but I am very ready to believe that the church, for all those to whom it makes effective appeal, is the greatest of all safeguards against such misery as comes from lack of friends. Unfortunately, there remain the unchurched who do not hear this appeal, or for whom, though they hear, it has no particular meaning.

Fraternal societies and clubs, trade unions and other social organizations, play a large part in the prophylaxis of misery, whatever other functions they may intend to perform. But in spite of all such socializing agencies there are in cheap hotels and lodging houses, in temporary homes and shelters, in boarding-houses, and as lodgers in tenements, a host of individuals who are stranded in this sense. They have no physical disability; they are not entirely without income; they are fairly adjusted, it may be, so far as their employment is concerned; but they suffer from a social maladjustment in that they have not made friends. Some few of them shrink from companionship and cherish their privacy, but the greater number of them await only opportunity to set in operation those all but universal and natural interchanges of courtesy and good-will

OUT OF FRIENDS

from which acquaintance and friendship inevitably spring.

Among those who have taken a friendly, coöperative interest — which I much appreciate — in the selection of topics to be considered in this discussion, and who have suggested that to my three particular Outs, — Out of Health, Out of Work, Out of Friends, — I add various other Outs, — such as Out of School, Out of Society, Out of Favor, — there is one who has insisted that there is at least one other loss deserving of more than passing mention, viz., Out of Heart. It is his thought that a man can come through any difficulties and deprivations if he but keep up his courage; that fear is the only foeman capable of doing mortal injury to the human spirit. I wish that I had the time and the insight to develop this theme. Out of heart, as I see it, does not always result from fear. It may result rather from lack of ambition, from that apathy and numbness which may be due to privation rather than to any original lack of spirit. To put heart into the poor is to give them both ambition and courage, and this I suppose is the true function of friendship.

Suicide, friendless old age, unemployment under ordinary industrial conditions, some forms of insanity and other disabling disease, immorality and crime, owe a part of their prevalence and their virulence to this absence of the capacity or opportunity for personal friendship, to the absence of those social props and safeguards which our friends naturally supply. The almshouse is the final apotheosis of friendlessness.

IV

Recognizing all this, and much that I have not even hinted as to the power of personal influence to transform human lives, there has been developed as a feature of organized charity a systematic scheme of friendly visiting among the poor. The friendly visitor is the man or woman who goes to a family that is in distress, not to carry them relief, or to solve their immediate specific problem as a district agent might have to do, but in order to establish a more permanent relation, in order to become a neighbor, interested in their affairs, sharing their troubles, sympathizing with them in adversity and in prosperity, representing them before the charitable societies when necessary, or before the courts, or before employers, or wherever else they may need a friend to stand by them.

Now the poor need friends. We shall not quarrel surely about that. They need other things also, as I have tried to show. They need health, they need homes, they need protection, they need leisure, they need regularity of income, they need insurance against certain contingencies, they need the conditions which permit a higher standard of living, they need education; and as a means to all these things and in response to a deep-seated universal social instinct which demands satisfaction, even when physical wants are not fully supplied, they need friends.

About a year ago I had some part — a very modest part indeed — in a discussion as to whether the friendly visiting scheme, as organized charity has conceived and carried it out, is the best way of meeting that need. Professor Patten had made [1] what seemed to me then and seems to me now a very interesting and important discovery,— that what the poor need most from the well-to-do and cultured classes is not more neighborliness, but better citizenship; not so much an altruism of volunteer personal service, as an income altruism that will create more favorable conditions of living; not so much personal sympathy for the misfortunes and hardships of some one family, valuable as that is, as an intelligent understanding of the misfortunes and hardships which many families encounter, and an effective sympathy with them in their attempts to rise to a level in which those misfortunes will occur less frequently and those hardships will be less in evidence. It was his idea that, if working and living conditions become

[1] Who is the Good Neighbor? In *Charities and the Commons*, XIX, 1642.

OUT OF FRIENDS

tolerable, acquaintance and friendship will spring up spontaneously among those who are naturally neighbors, who are thrown into ordinary industrial and social relations. This is not to say that personal friendships must forever be founded upon the accidents of birth or income or education. We all know instances to the contrary — instances which are prophetic of a better social order when there shall be freer mingling among all sorts and conditions of men. The question which Professor Patten raised is not at all as to the possibility of such an exceptional personal relation, or as to its beauty or its value for both sides, but rather as to the relative value, in a broad programme of social work, of an organized system of friendly visiting which enlists visitors on one side of a line, and lists the visited on the other side, and adjusts the one to the other by a process essentially arbitrary and artificial, however skilful the adjustment may be and however accurate the psychological analysis both of the visitor and of the visited, upon which the adjustment is based.

The question, I repeat, is not about the value of friendship, but about the way to secure it. I confess that it is my own strong conviction that the provision of neighborhood facilities for spontaneous social intercourse, the shortening of hours, the raising of wages, the improvement of health, and other similar methods,

MISERY AND ITS CAUSES

will prove more productive of the best kind of neighborliness and mutual personal service, than all the efforts consciously directed towards that specific end.

The lesson of this maladjustment is therefore like that of the others which we have considered. The remedies that we find to be indicated are the remedies for the other kinds of misery. The faith upon which we may stand is the faith which has inspired our policies for dealing with health problems and industrial problems. The confidence which it implies in the soundness of human nature and its responsiveness to generous treatment is again put in contrast with the pessimistic view that to be friendless is to be without the latent capacity for friendship. That faith assumes in its democracy that there is the same capacity among the poor as among others to make friends, to choose their friends, to be friends, as well as to be befriended.

CHAPTER V

THE ADVERSE CONDITIONS IN DEPENDENT FAMILIES

I

WHEN I was ready to write these lectures, I did, first of all, what I have long made it a profitable practice to do under similar circumstances. I called our staff of district agents into a sort of confidential consultation; and on this occasion I put to them the straight question which I am here trying to answer. Asking them to disregard for the moment all that they had read about the causes of poverty, and all that I or any one had tried to teach them, I demanded their own personal impressions as to the immediate causes, the actual present moving causes, of such distress as they encounter in the homes of the poor.

The first said ignorance and overcrowding and low wages, especially in work done at home. Cross-examined closely, she insisted that it was her deliberate opinion that either by increasing income, or by giving enough time and attention to counteract their ignorance of things which they ought to know, in almost every family under her care most of the hardships which she encountered could be made to disappear. The second said that in a very small proportion of instances the distress is due to the fault of the individual himself, but that in far the greater proportion it is due to some outside cause, to environmental conditions, such, for example, as an inability to find work at remunerative wages. A third said that ignorance of matters directly affecting the physical welfare and the care of the family was the most prominent cause of misery, and another attributed it to the kind of work that people are doing. Another said hard conditions, and another ignorance, having changed her earlier impression that lack of ambition was the great failing. Another indorsed the first answer — ignorance, overcrowding, and low wages — and added physical disability and industrial maladjustment. Still another gave her voice for ignorance, and a preference, especially among foreigners, for remaining in certain undesirable occupations. Another said lack of employment, and still another ignorance and physical handicap. Another said that the unpreparedness of women to make a home was the chief evil. The last vote of all was again for ignorance, but not this time so much the ignorance of the poor, that is, of those who suffer, as the ignorance of the rest of us, the effects of whose actions recoil upon them. One objector expressed doubt as to whether ignorance was so much at fault as will power, suggesting that knowledge without strength and opportunity only adds to

THE ADVERSE CONDITIONS

the suffering. It was the idea of this agent that the environment of the great mass of human beings is distinctly unfavorable to the development of the higher qualities and the attainment of the higher ideals, and that those who succeed often do so through the display of what are really ignoble and questionable traits.

The most striking thing about this concurrent testimony is its wide departure from conventional discussions of poverty. There is not a word about drink, not a word about unwise philanthropy, not a word about laziness, not a word even about lack of work, although this discussion occurred in the midst of a winter when every agent was overworked because of the large number of applications from those who were out of work. Ignorance and sheer incapacity are so nearly universal and so much a matter of course that they are not ordinarily named in the records, and yet are so obvious and so serious that they arise at once in the minds of workers when they are directly challenged to give their impressions.

I have before me a personal letter, written soon after the stimulating discussion in agents' meeting by one who had taken part in it. This letter, as the writer says, is disjointed. It does not set out to be philosophical or scientific. It begins with a paragraph which I shall not quote, expressing the conviction that if we could have one generation sober we would have gone a long

MISERY AND ITS CAUSES

way toward solving the problem of poverty, and that brotherly love, religiously carried out, would pretty nearly take us the rest of the way. I need not take you to a district agent's letter to learn the value of religion and temperance. You will agree with her or disagree with her about such matters according to your own previous convictions and your bringing up, and so we pass that over. But the writer has painted a picture which, disjointed and inartistic as it is, I present as it is drawn, complete in its very incompleteness, the more convincing that it is a bit inarticulate.

"Ignorance," she says, "not necessarily a lack of book learning, is one of the prime causes of poverty — ignorance of all that goes to make up life. A child reared in a very poor home has to go to work before he should. He drudges away and adds his little mite to the family budget. He is underfed and improperly fed; he has had no child life, and finally he tires of putting all his wage into the house and not having money to handle; he meets a girl who has probably a similar story to tell; they marry, thinking to better their condition, neither of them having anything like the knowledge that one should possess to enter into that bond; neither have they any regard as to whether they are physically fit to marry; no cash saved, not even reasonably sure of an income. They buy their household effects on the instalment plan, and before they have had time to pay for them the husband loses his work; in the meantime the wife has had them both insured; that runs behind — the majority of the

THE ADVERSE CONDITIONS

poor starve themselves that they may be in a position to have a decent burial; their rent piles up; they have had to pinch and save and run in debt to get food of any description; their bodies have been undernourished; they may have their rooms in a basement because the rent is cheap; one or the other contracts rheumatism; the wife becomes pregnant; a midwife or a maternity hospital confines her; she does not get the proper food or after attention; they get their pint of beer to help strengthen her, — probably a doctor has prescribed it to help produce milk, — both have probably been brought up to its use, have never heard of its bad effects; they cannot believe that the same amount of cash invested in milk would nourish them better; one or both drift into the drinking habit. She gets careless; she scarcely weans the baby until another is on the way; she has never been taught her duty as a mother; she cannot recall any early training or example in this direction; she has no sense of responsibility; no resources in time of adversity; she has a lack of fine principles; lacks frugality; would not think of saving her pennies but waits until she can get a dollar; that time never comes; she has no apparent pride in herself, home, or husband; does not understand how to make the most of things; she has inherited a moral weakness; lacks will power and control; she cannot see that she is losing her grip, so to speak, on her husband — if she ever had any; she is discouraged and is beginning to show the strain; the second child fares worse than the first; she has not been taught how to prepare meals properly; she has no idea of the kind of food which is most wholesome; she has no time to prepare a meal, having spent the morning hours in gossip with neighbors; she runs to the delicatessen store and pays two or three times as much for an improperly cooked dish as it is worth and serves it cold; it is not conducive to her husband's comfort, health, or temper; the table is rarely ever set; there is no table linen; food is pitched on the table; she looks like distress; the children look worse and are slapped in the face and banged about, — in short, her home life with her husband is worse than her parental home was. The husband gets sick; if he goes to the dispensary and gets medicine he does not follow it up and take the medicine as he should — they lack that great essential, thoroughness. He returns to work too soon; finally is handicapped by disease of some kind which prevents his working as usual, but the babies continue to come with perfect regularity. Immorality in the home results from crowded conditions; children see what is not fit for their eyes and early begin practices ruinous to them and to those with whom they come in contact. Children are conceived while their parents are drunk — they learn the taste of drink with their mother's milk. What can be expected of the outcome? The mother knows nothing of her duty as a mother; she, too, is run down in health; the children have not had half a chance; and as soon as they are large enough history repeats itself, and so it goes."

Some superficial social students will be ready to stop right here. "These families are made up," I hear them say, "according to your own testimony, of ignorant, inefficient people. They are getting as much as they earn, and if it is not enough to live on, there is

THE ADVERSE CONDITIONS

nothing for it but to help them out as we are doing with a little charitable relief, take their children into asylums, their sick into hospitals, their old and worn-out into the almshouse, and make the best of it." But I reply that is not making the best of it. That is taking the line which is of least resistance only because the ruts are deep with long travel along that line. It is the line neither of least natural resistance, nor of science, nor yet of common sense.

If there is any one evil that is easy to overcome, it is ignorance. If there is any one misfortune from which it is both just and feasible to relieve mankind, it is ignorance. If there is any one serious mistake in the letter which I have quoted, it is in the statement that "history repeats itself, and so it goes." To me it is not a ground for pessimism, but for very confident optimism, to discover that what is wrong with my brother is nothing worse than ignorance. Do I not know that others, no better than he, have overcome ignorance, and that under proper conditions he also will overcome it? Let any man who despairs of the capacity of the poor to rise from their poverty seek other explanation than that they are ignorant and incapable. This first fragmentary testimony is not discouraging, but distinctly promising.

II

An experienced district agent[1] has recently spent more than a year as a fellow in the School of Philanthropy in a careful, intensive study of five hundred families who had been for some period under the continuous oversight and care of the Society's district committees. She distinguishes among the families seven different types, classified according to the characteristics of the principal breadwinner in the family. (Diagram 6.)

There were, first, the families who were in some temporary difficulty, shown to be temporary not only by the appearance of things at the time of their application, but by the subsequent history. These difficulties were usually either of unemployment or of acute illness, circumstances for which the head of the family, in the absence of any general scheme of insurance against these casualties, can hardly be held responsible. There were 109 of these cases, or about twenty-two per cent of the whole number. There was, second, the

[1] Miss Caroline Goodyear, of the New York Charity Organization Society.

THE ADVERSE CONDITIONS

non-support type, including all cases in which distinct blame attaches to the man for his failure to support his

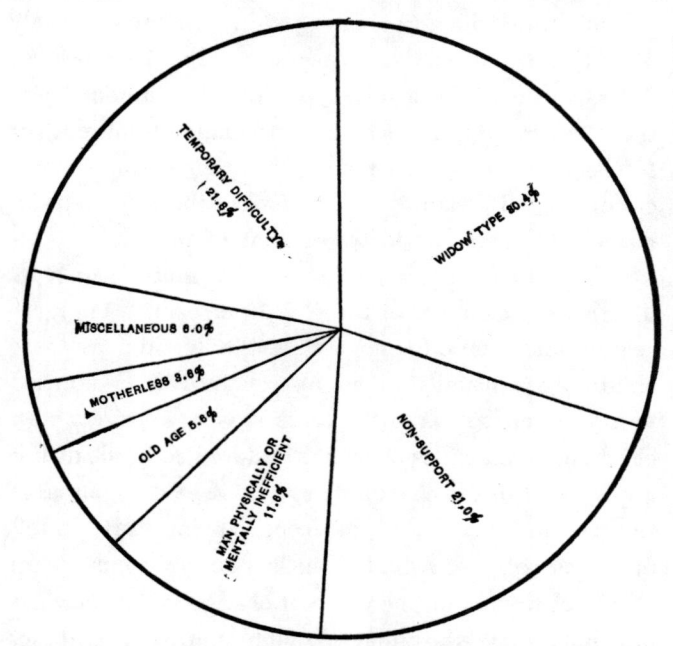

Pie chart with the following segments: WIDOW TYPE 30.4%, NON-SUPPORT 21.0%, MAN PHYSICALLY OR MENTALLY INEFFICIENT 11.0%, OLD AGE 5.6%, MOTHERLESS 3.6%, MISCELLANEOUS 6.0%, TEMPORARY DIFFICULTY 21.0%

DIAGRAM 6. Types among 500 families under the care of the Charity Organization Society of the City of New York.

household; there were 105 of these cases, or twenty-one per cent of the five hundred. There were, third, the well-disposed but physically or mentally inefficient, men willing to work and showing that willingness by every

[175]

reasonable test, but incapable at best of earning a sufficient support for the family, easily thrown out of employment, and hard to restore to it. There were only 58 of these families, twelve per cent of the five hundred. There was next the widow type, including among these the cases in which the man is permanently absent, or totally disabled by tuberculosis or other chronic physical or mental disability. These were the most numerous — 152 cases, or thirty per cent of the whole. Affording a direct contrast to these is the motherless type. There were eighteen of these, 3.6 per cent. They are seldom under care for a great length of time, as these children are usually taken by relatives or committed to an institution. For the same reason widowers with children, and families of orphan children, as a rule do not apply at all to the charitable agencies. Old age marks the type in 28 cases, 5.6 per cent, leaving thirty in all, or six per cent, for a final miscellaneous group, made up chiefly of women on the verge of old age and of families in which mothers, either through marked moral degeneracy or otherwise, signally fail in their responsibilities, leaving the home a travesty, as the investigator puts it, of the motherless type, and forming the typical case for the Society for the Prevention of Cruelty to Children.

This classification, as you will see, was not devised to establish any thesis, nor does it pretend to be an analy-

THE ADVERSE CONDITIONS

sis of the causes of poverty. Experienced social workers recognize even from this brief description not only the types that I have enumerated, but also the course of treatment fairly well indicated for each of the typical cases. The temporary difficulties of the first group, where there is acute illness of the wage earner or genuine unemployment without other serious complications, may require temporary relief, with cautious safeguards against the forming of a habit of dependence. A tonic rather than a palliative is required. The non-support cases require discipline; the physically or mentally inefficient require medical care and special attention such as is perhaps best illustrated thus far by the employment bureau for the handicapped; the widow and fatherless children are likely to require permanent, liberal, and regular relief; the motherless family is fortunate if there is a near relative of the father, or a daughter old enough to assume the responsibility for the household; while old age, in the absence of any general system of old-age pensions, points as a rule to care in a permanent home, although there are adventurous spirits who favor a boarding-out system, such as has been found in some states to be a satisfactory substitute for institutional care in the case of children.

III

I have thought that it would be a contribution to a preventive and constructive programme in social work to make a somewhat careful study of the conspicuous characteristics of a large group of dependent families, of the respects in which they and their circumstances are different from other families and their circumtances, and equally of the respects in which they are not different, based upon case records and contemporaneously recorded observations and impressions. It has appeared to me that such an analysis would throw light upon the conditions which accompany destitution and give to those who are able to draw their own conclusions some basis for inference concerning the causes of poverty and the measures which are indicated for its prevention.

I have therefore made an inquiry into the conditions present in five thousand families who came under the care of the district committees of the Charity Organization Society in the two years ending September 30, 1908.

We know these families at best only superficially. Even so we find without difficulty all those well-defined

THE ADVERSE CONDITIONS

manifestations of misery which we have been considering, not isolated, but in combination one with another and with others less obtrusive. The hardships and disadvantageous conditions which we discern clearly go far towards explaining their present misery and far towards accounting for the emergence of the particular classes of unfortunates in isolation to whom we have referred. If we could know them well enough, if we could know more intimately the handicaps of body and the subtler defects of personality which they have inherited, the deficiencies of their education, the unfavorable industrial conditions which have been imposed upon them, we might then be able to speak with more assurance as to the relative importance of the causes which are operating to produce poverty, dependence, and misery. The Rockefeller Institute is working with this in view in the particular field of preventive medicine. In the larger field of social misery there are precisely similar opportunities for those who approach its specific problems in the same spirit.

The records of these five thousand families were examined for all the information they contained in regard to the constitution and the circumstances of the families at the time of their application for assistance, including also, of course, such well-defined permanent characteristics as must have been a part of the situation at that time. No attempt has been made to decide in each case, with the aid of a prearranged list of possible causes, which one was the cause of dependence in that particular family on that particular occasion.[1] Our interest is not in the psychology of the tabulators, but in the facts about the families; and on the basis of the facts discovered about these families, not in the first visit, but in the course of the Society's entire acquaintance with them, it is possible to describe the conditions which existed at the critical period when the family, of its own initiative or through the offices of a friend, came to us for help.

[1] The Causes of Poverty: by Lilian Brandt. In *Political Science Quarterly*, XXIII, No. 4.

IV

What were these five thousand families like? How do they differ from the "normal family" we all have in our minds?

There are among them representatives of all the types of misery that we have discussed. Two men and one woman committed suicide; four men and two women are known to have tried to do so. There are criminals among them, ranging from the young German, less than a year in the country, who, as if playing the part of a popular newspaper character, stole a little food for his wife and baby; through the so-called petty offenders — "drunk and disorderlies," wife beaters, men who consistently avoid supporting their families, and petty thieves — who form the bulk of the criminals in these families; to an occasional forger, burglar, blackmailer, murderer — a young clerk, for example, to cite another newspaper type, in prison because he has shot a girl with whom he was infatuated, leaving his wife and two children dependent.

There are old people among them, waiting for death to make room for them in one of the private homes for the aged. There are others who will go, less reluctantly, it is good to remember, than their predecessors went ten years ago, to the City Home for the Aged and Infirm.

Some of the children were already in institutions, put there by parents as the first resort when their hard times came; others will be sent because their parents are not fit guardians. There are insane and feeble-minded and epileptic, and blind, and lame, and crooked. Practically all of the families are familiar with hospitals and dispensaries. There are men and women, a few, living together illegally. There are a few young women, alone, with illegitimate children.

It should be kept in mind for a background that these are in the main American families either by birth or by long residence. (Diagrams 7 and 8.) They are not, therefore, as a body, laboring under the disadvantage of recent arrival in the country, and in this respect they differ from some of the other groups of dependent families in New York City. For this reason, however, they are more typical of the poor of American cities than the entire body of dependent families in New York would be. For this reason also, their other disabilities can be seen in truer proportions than if they were dwarfed, as they frequently are in popular considerations of the poor of New York, by the assumption that most of them are recent immigrants, all of whose troubles may be traced to that fact.

THE ADVERSE CONDITIONS

Only 240 had been less than a year in the city when they applied for assistance, and of these 66 were

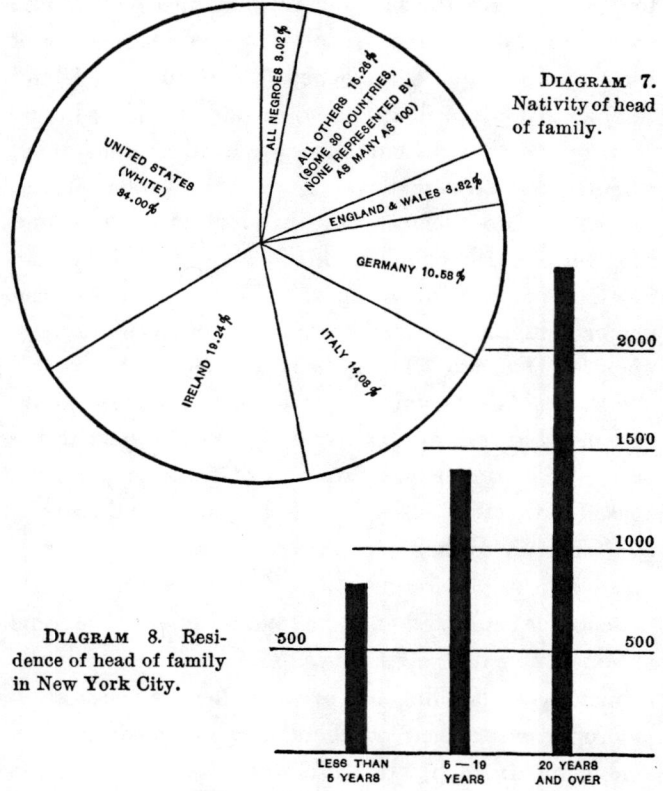

DIAGRAM 7. Nativity of head of family.

UNITED STATES (WHITE) 54.00%
ALL NEGROES 3.02%
ALL OTHERS 15.26% (SOME 30 COUNTRIES, NONE REPRESENTED BY AS MANY AS 100)
ENGLAND & WALES 3.82%
GERMANY 10.58%
ITALY 14.08%
IRELAND 19.24%

DIAGRAM 8. Residence of head of family in New York City.

LESS THAN 5 YEARS | 5—19 YEARS | 20 YEARS AND OVER

native Americans, while some of the foreign-born had been living already for a number of years in other parts

[183]

of this country. About one-sixth of them altogether had lived in New York less than five years; over a fourth from five to twenty years, and nearly half had lived here at least twenty years. (Diagram 8.) Most of them, in other words, have been on Manhattan Island sufficiently long to justify them in calling it their home.

In over a third of our cases the head of the family, whether man or woman, was born in the United States; in twenty-three per cent the head of the family had been born and lived all his life in New York City. In nineteen per cent he was born in Ireland, in fourteen per cent in Italy; in ten and a half per cent in Germany. (Diagram 7.) In the two years covered by this study the Italians gained perceptibly upon the Irish, and they bid fair, at an early date, to come next to the native-born among our families. Of course percentages of nationalities mean nothing at all as to their relative tendency toward dependence unless the number of those who apply for help at different places is complete and is compared with the total number of the same nationality in the population. The Irish, for example, furnish many families, not because there is necessarily, in proportion to their numbers, exceptional destitution among the Irish, but because New York is to a large extent an Irish city. Russians and Austrians do not appear among our families because Russian and Aus-

THE ADVERSE CONDITIONS

trian Jews apply instead to the United Hebrew Charities. To make any generalization concerning German dependence we would need to take into account both applications to the German Society and the total German population of the city. It must always be remembered that the five thousand families are not necessarily representative even of Greater New York, for the reason that the residents of three of the five boroughs, Brooklyn, Queens, and Richmond, are excluded. It may be of interest, however, to record that some thirty-five nationalities were represented among them, including Arabia, China, Japan, India, Syria, and our own Philippine Islands.

The next significant thing about these families is that a large proportion of them are not normally constituted families. (Diagram 9.)

There are twelve families of orphans, children left without either father or mother, and unable, because they are too young or too inexperienced or too delicate, to earn enough among them to keep together without assistance.

There are next 162 cases in which there is no woman at the head of the family, 54 of these being single men, 94 widowers, and fourteen deserted husbands. I should say in passing that men or women who are technically "homeless" are cared for in the Joint Application

MISERY AND ITS CAUSES

Bureau, and as most single men and some women are without shelter or are living at a lodging house when they

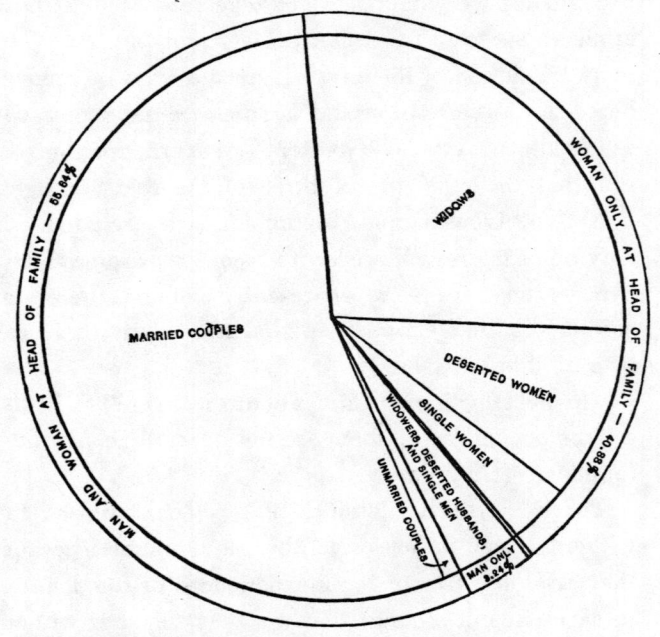

DIAGRAM 9. Family status.
(The narrow section between Single Women and Widowers represents Orphans, .24%.)

ask for charitable assistance they do not as a rule come under the care of the districts, and are therefore not represented in this study in the proportions they occupy in the dependent population of the city. Most of the

THE ADVERSE CONDITIONS

widowers and deserted husbands had children under twenty-one, five of them had each five under fourteen.

This group, like the orphan children, is a small proportion of the total five thousand cases. The next group, however, the cases in which there is no male head of the family, consists of 2044 cases, four-tenths of the whole number. Seven hundred and eighty-five of these were single women or widows or deserted women who had no children under twenty-one years of age, but there were 1248 widows and divorced, separated and deserted women with from one to eight children under twenty-one — in most cases at least one under fourteen, in 103, five or more — and eleven young unmarried women with illegitimate children. One of the widows was a young Italian woman with four little children, whose husband had been murdered the day before, but most of the widowhood was not recent at the time of application, while on the other hand most of the desertion was recent. In less than twenty-five per cent of the cases of widows had the husband been dead less than a year, while the deserting husband had been away less than a year in sixty per cent and less than a month in thirty per cent of the cases.

These families deprived by death or desertion of their natural head are a constant large class among dependent families. Over one-fourth of the five thousand are widows; one-tenth are deserted women. Half of the widows and four-fifths of the deserted women have little children dependent upon them. In Manhattan and Bronx boroughs widows constitute a little over four per cent of the total population; they constitute nearly seven per cent of the individuals making up these families.

Comparing the numbers just given with those quoted from the earlier study it will be seen that there is a close correspondence. The total number of families in which there is a woman at the head is naturally a larger proportion of the whole than those that are distinguished as the widowhood type, but the proportion in which there is actually a widow at the head of the family is a little less than Miss Goodyear's calculation shows, since, looking at the family from the standpoint of treatment, she has very naturally included cases in which the male head of the family is totally disabled or has been for some time away from the family so that the treatment to be given approximates that which would naturally be given to the widow with children. The two studies then, relating to different periods, the one intensive and the other extensive, bring us to the same generalization, that about one-third of all our families are widows with children or families that are practically in their position.

It is on behalf of these families that there has recently arisen a demand for a reconsideration of the policy

THE ADVERSE CONDITIONS

which now prevails on the time-honored but with us, practically for a third of a century, closed subject of public out-door relief. While prohibiting, at first gradually and piecemeal and finally by a charter provision, the giving of public out-door relief in the homes of the poor, whether in the form of groceries, or coal, or money, we have pursued a very liberal policy with reference to the care of children in institutions. In the case of certain institutions, of late years a larger number than before, the municipal authorities have paid institutions for the care of children, even though they were actually boarded outside the walls of the institution in private families, provided these were other families than those in which the children originally belonged. Some of those who are vehemently opposed to the institutional care of children and others who are alarmed lest the burden upon the private relief societies may soon become greater than they can bear — if it is not already so — are beginning to protest that it would be more logical and consistent to pay the mothers of these children for their maintenance in their own homes, or possibly, as a halfway measure, to permit the institutions to which children are committed to use the money which is now paid to them in maintaining these children in their own homes, provided they are good homes, rather than in the homes of strangers. There are undoubtedly two sides to this question, or perhaps more than two. I point out merely that the departure from payment for institutional care which we have already made, slight as it is, breaks down the traditional division of work between public and private charity; and on the other hand, that the very large sum now raised annually by the charitable societies for the relief of the poor in their homes — more than a million dollars a year — would be endangered by any system of public relief of the poor in their homes even though it were limited to widows with children. Those who favor public relief for widows with children, as an alternative for institutional care, should face the probability that it must become also a substitute for a very considerable part of the private relief which is now provided. A longer look ahead may possibly discover yet other substitutes for both public and private relief. Indemnity in cases of accident, sickness, old age, and even unemployment, through insurance, to the cost of which the insured have contributed, is a policy which is to be preferred to charitable relief on grounds both of justice and of expediency.

We find, then, among these five thousand families a very few cases in which there is no head of the family; we find a small number, not much over three per cent, consisting of a man alone or with dependent children; we find a larger number, forty-one per cent, consisting

THE ADVERSE CONDITIONS

of a woman alone, or with children dependent on her; and we come, finally, to the cases in which there are both a man and a woman at the head of the family. There are 2782 of these, forty of them, however, not married, and in 476 cases there are no children under twenty-one. Of normally constituted families, therefore, in the ordinary sense of married couples with children still at home, there are among our five thousand dependent families only 2277, or forty-six per cent.

V

The next conspicuous characteristic of these families, after the fact that a large proportion of them are mere mutilated fragments of families, is the large number of small children. The five thousand families contained 19,504 individuals, and of these 9172, nearly half, were children under fourteen years of age. In the general population of the state of New York children under fourteen form twenty-seven per cent of the total; young persons between fourteen and twenty-one, twelve and one half per cent; and the adult population twenty-one years of age and over, amounts to sixty per cent. In these five thousand dependent families the corresponding percentages are forty-seven, instead of twenty-seven, under fourteen years of age; nine, instead of twelve and one-half, between fourteen and twenty-one; and forty-four, instead of sixty and one-half, adult. In other words, the abnormal proportion of small children is counterbalanced by a small proportion both of older children and of adults. This does not indicate unusually large families, but the absence which we have already noted, of the full quota of male heads, and an unusual proportion of young families. (Diagram 10.)

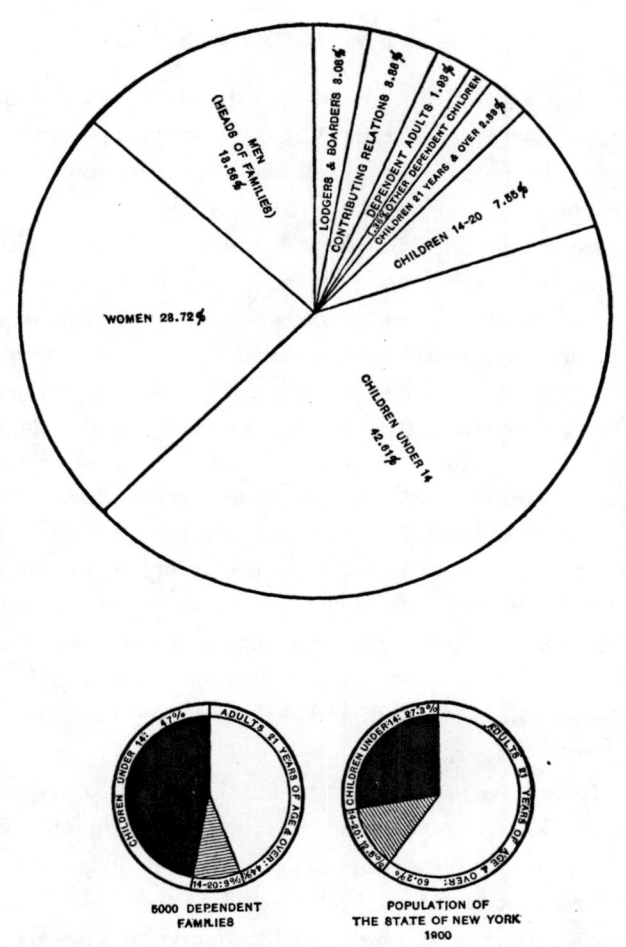

DIAGRAM 10. Composition of households; and composition of families in comparison with the general population of the State of New York.

[193]

MISERY AND ITS CAUSES

The age of the head of the family tells the same story. (Diagram 11.) If we group ages in five-year periods, we shall find the maximum in the period from thirty-five to forty, the age in which there is normally the largest number of small children. There is among these families a curve similar to that which has been noticed in the life of an individual, the reverse of what has been called the curve of economic prosperity. Our line rises steadily from twenty to forty; descending from this maximum by regular stages until the number between fifty-five and sixty approximates that between twenty and twenty-five; after which, in old age, it rises again, and there are six hundred families, sometimes, of course, a single aged man or woman, in which the head is over sixty years of age. The descending line between forty and sixty represents in the individual family the improvement resulting from the growth of children and their assuming the burdens of wage earners.

In size, we have said, these families are not conspicuous. The average number of individuals in our five thousand families was four, including lodgers and boarders and relatives, both dependent and contributing. So far as our records indicate, 1332 individuals belonging to these families were away from home at the time of the application — in hospitals, institutions for children,

THE ADVERSE CONDITIONS

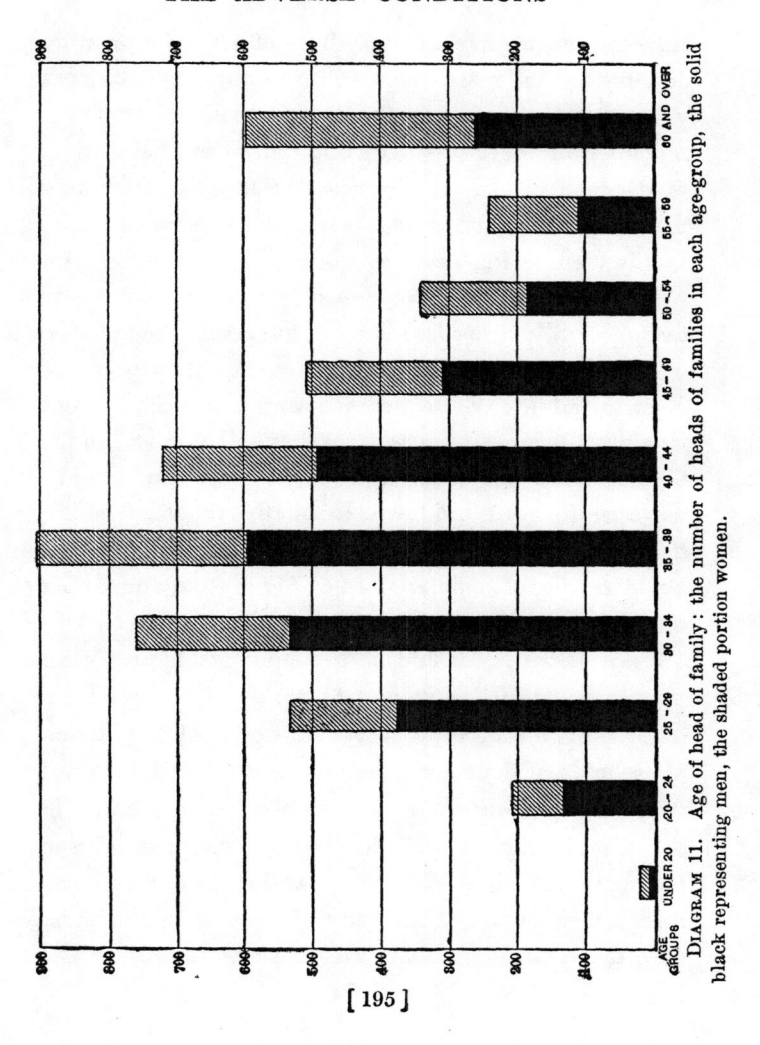

DIAGRAM 11. Age of head of family: the number of heads of families in each age-group, the solid black representing men, the shaded portion women.

prisons, insane asylums, or in another city or even country for one reason or another — but these absences were more than offset by the 2072 individuals who were members of the household, but not, strictly speaking, of the family. In other words, the families, including members away from home, average 3.9 persons to the family; while the average size of the household with which we are directly concerned is an even four. The average for "private families" in the general population of Manhattan and Bronx boroughs in 1900 was 4.5. Even the addition of the deceased and deserted husbands would not bring our figure up to that. "Family," in the Census terminology, is almost identical with "household" as we use the word, and the size of our five thousand households follows quite closely the size of the 433,953 households in which the population of Manhattan and Bronx boroughs was distributed in 1900. (Diagram 12.) In both cases the household of three persons figures most prominently. It is followed in our families by households of two and of four; in the general population households of four are more numerous than those of two. Households of one person are less numerous in the Census figures than in ours, because a person temporarily with friends or boarding would be enumerated as part of that "family"; and in the same way the large households are more numerous in the

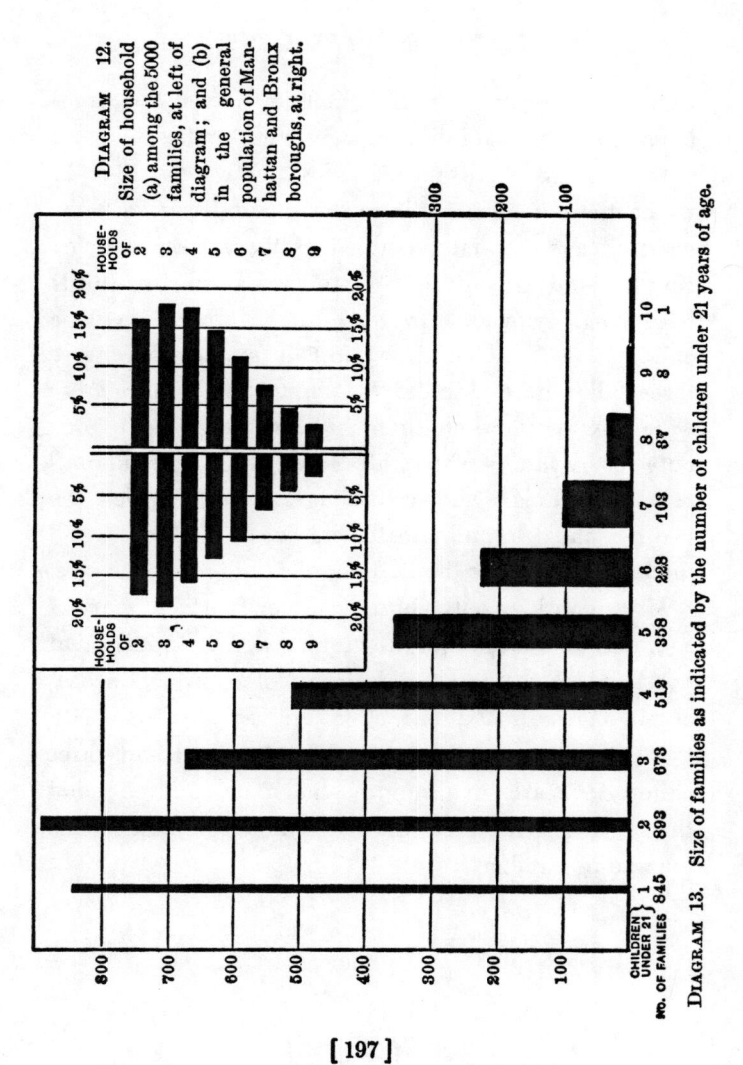

DIAGRAM 12. Size of household (a) among the 5000 families, at left of diagram; and (b) in the general population of Manhattan and Bronx boroughs, at right.

DIAGRAM 13. Size of families as indicated by the number of children under 21 years of age.

MISERY AND ITS CAUSES

Census figures, because they include hotels, boarding-houses, schools, and other congregate families.

Of our five thousand families there were 1342 in which there were no children at all under twenty-one years of age; about one-third of these were married couples, and all but sixty of the remaining two-thirds were single women. In 845 families there was one child; in 893, two children; in 673 families there were three children; and in the remaining 1247 families there were four or more children, reaching a climax in one noteworthy family of ten, all under twenty-one, and all at home. This is shown in Diagram 13, in which the width of the column indicates the size of the family, and the height indicates the number of families of each size.

If we consider only children under fourteen years of age, that is, under the legal working age, it appears that one-third of the families were childless in this sense; about one-sixth had one child, and another one-sixth two children; approximately seven hundred had three children; nearly five hundred had four children; and the remaining families had five or more, nine being the maximum number.

VI

Our five thousand families are fundamentally handicapped as a group, from an economic point of view, by widowhood and desertion and by an unusual proportion of young children. They exhibit also many other disabilities: physical and moral, as individuals and as families; inherent and accidental; personal and environmental; economic and social; temporary and permanent; curable and ineradicable.

Under twenty-five headings we have put down all the adverse conditions which we know were present at the time of the application for assistance and which were sufficiently tangible and definite to be classified, including those already mentioned and including all the defects of character which, whether or not they were in evidence at that particular time, are known to have been an element in the situation. Some of these disabilities are such natural and inevitable experiences as spring from widowhood, childbirth, large families, and old age — not in themselves causes of poverty in well-regulated families and in well-regulated communities, but nevertheless genuine disabilities under the circumstances in which they are encountered in our New York tenements. Others are such exceptional misfortunes as have always touched the fountains of compassion — an acute illness, death by violence, physical deformity, mental afflictions, domestic tragedy. Others have their origin more directly in our industrial system, or farther back in its financial foundation. The failure of a Trust Company precipitates—of course I do not mean causes—an economic disturbance, for which frenzied finance, a bad banking system, and worse banking practice have prepared the way, and straightway shops close, railway cars are idle, building operations cease, and for two years or more families in the tenements of New York are in need of food and clothing and money to pay their rent. This appears in our table of disabilities as unemployment — a barbarous word, as my critics frequently protest, but I tell them rather a barbarous fact for which there is no pretty word, and the barbarity of the word, which already has ample authority for its use both in England and America, troubles me much less than the barbarity of the fact. Distress due to unemployment resulting directly from the faulty judgment and the reprehensible practices of financiers and other business men is a form of that maladjustment which I hold to be responsible for so large a part of our poverty.

In the disabilities to which I have referred there may

THE ADVERSE CONDITIONS

always be an element of personal weakness, a certain congenital tendency it may be towards dependence, a weakness at this point of the resisting power which gives entrance to the full force and influence of the disability. That is to say, another family might also have lost its principal breadwinner, and not come to actual poverty as a result. Old age might have brought to others only dignified retirement and comfortable leisure. Others might have had large broods of children without the pinch of hunger, and the advent of each child, under other more favorable circumstances, might not have prompted an application for charitable assistance. Illness, deformity, insanity, and domestic tragedy do not always mean dependence, and it is true, as I have said repeatedly, that we have no complete diagnosis of the dependence until we have examined the heredity and the mental and physical qualities of the individual, as well as the particular circumstances which seem to have brought the family into its present trouble. In so far as personal infirmities of character have been revealed in the course of our acquaintance we have taken them into account. These are the cases in which there is a present or previous criminal record, in the technical sense, in which there is evidence of immorality, in which there are wayward and incorrigible children, in which there is cruelty and abuse by the husband, or definite evidence of non-support of his family, or actual desertion of wife and children. Even a violent temper or excessive irritability are put down — not in malice, but in charity, in order that we may fully understand what the disabilities are with which we have to deal.

Under some twenty-five headings, then, from widowhood to gambling, from rheumatism to unreliability, from recent arrival in New York to a residence of sixty years on earth, we have put them all down. We have not sought to say in any one case that widowhood, or unemployment, or intemperance, or accident, or shiftlessness, or any other specific disability, is the sole cause or the chief cause or the contributing cause of the poverty, but we have put down every such disability without exaggeration or prejudice in order that they may be considered *en masse* and in isolation, in the several independent instances and in their relation to one another.

VII

Let us first run over these twenty-five disabilities in the order of their numerical importance, without regard to natural groupings, beginning with the smallest figures, at the bottom of the column in the table on page 204.

In twenty-two of the five thousand families, less than one-half of one per cent, there is a definite record of gambling. In nearly one per cent children under fourteen years of age were working for money at the time of application; not ordinarily in violation of the law, but running errands or selling papers after school hours and on Saturday, or out of school altogether acting as nurse-maid, though there are instances of a thirteen-year-old Italian girl who was a cigar-stripper, a little Russian finisher, and an American telegraph messenger. Small as this percentage is, it illustrates the misplaced thrift that is less than a virtue, and forms a contrast to the laziness and shiftlessness that are a larger item among the fathers and mothers.

A disposition to beg was noted in two per cent of the families, more frequently on the part of the woman

MISERY AND ITS CAUSES

The principal disabilities present in five thousand dependent families in New York City

Disabilities	Number of Individuals Affected	Families Number	Per Cent
1. Unemployment	4424	3458	69.16
2. Overcrowding	—	2014	44.68[1]
3. Widowhood	—	1472	29.44
4. Chronic physical disability other than tuberculosis or rheumatism	1603	1365	27.30
5. Temporary physical disability other than accident or childbirth	1158	984	19.68
6. More than three children under fourteen	—	944	18.88
7. Intemperance	1000	833	16.66
8. Less than five years in New York City	—	814	16.28
9. Tuberculosis	675	619	12.38
10. Desertion and persistent non-support	—	606	12.12
11. Head of family sixty years old or more	—	599	11.98
12. Laziness, shiftlessness, etc.	667	588	11.76
13. Childbirth	363	363	7.26
14. Rheumatism	359	347	6.94
15. Immorality	337	256	5.12
16. Mental disease, defect, or deficiency	267	248	4.96
17. Cruelty, abuse, etc.	229	221	4.42
18. Accident	201	198	3.96
19. Untruthfulness, unreliability, etc.	210	194	3.88
20. Criminal record	161	151	3.02
21. Violent or irritable temper, etc.	148	140	2.80
22. Waywardness of children	160	129	2.58
23. Disposition to beg	134	117	2.34
24. Child labor (generally not illegal)	45	42	0.84
25. Gambling	22	22	0.44

[1] Based on the 4508 cases in which there was definite information on this point.

THE ADVERSE CONDITIONS

than of the man, as she is too generally the official representative of the family in its dealings with charitable agencies; and in two and a half per cent there were children who were unruly to the degree generally described as waywardness or incorrigibility. Of one Irish family it is recorded that all of the seven children "run wild, steal from wagons, etc."

A violent, morbid, irritable, quarrelsome, melancholy, disagreeable, obstinate, stubborn, complaining, unreasonable, excitable, nervous, reckless, impertinent, despondent, jealous, peculiar, or depressing, temper or disposition, not amounting to cruelty or well-recognized mental defect, was discernible in three per cent of the cases. This would be a small percentage of deviations from equability and poise in five thousand families unharassed by the immediate pressure of the rent problem, but the poor cannot afford to be cross or have the blues. Excuses could be found in many cases: irritability is frequently accompanied by illness; one girl who is described as "insolent and melancholy" had at the time three cases of tuberculosis in her family; a woman is said to be "jealous," whose husband supports other women instead of herself.

In three per cent, also, there was a criminal record. If men were relatively few, as they were, among the persons with abnormal dispositions, here they constitute almost the entire group. The offences most frequently noted are non-support, small thefts, and disorderly conduct, but there are a few clearly defined examples of bigamy and the other more serious crimes: one man had committed forgery and gone away with another woman, leaving a wife and eight children, five of them under fourteen; another had served three sentences for robbery; another is now in Sing Sing for nineteen years; another is an "anarchist on parole." From our point of view, however, the petty offences are equally serious, and the man who is "constantly in the work-house for non-support and intoxication," and still more the man who ought to be there for the same reasons but is not, may be really more harmful elements in their families and in the community than a criminal of passion.

Untruthfulness and unreliability are sufficiently serious to appear in the record in four per cent of the cases. This includes two instances of "inconsistent" women, which must be admitted to be an abnormally low proportion. Unreliability is sometimes accompanied by mental defect or by age, and may not always be a fault. Occasionally a woman is described as "reticent" or "evasive," or "not frank," but such are not included in this group, nor is the man who is said to be a "smooth talker." Here again, as in the case of faults of temper and a disposition to beg, the bulk of

THE ADVERSE CONDITIONS

the individuals concerned are women; and here again, it is not because the men are almost all upright and trustworthy, but because it is the statements of the women which we have the opportunity of testing.

In four per cent of all the families, also, some one was suffering from the effects of an accident at the time of the application. Over half the injured persons were men, and many of these had been hurt while at work; the women and children were more frequently suffering from a fall or some domestic mishap.

The cases of cruelty and abusiveness number about four and a half per cent, not including here desertion or mere non-support without other mistreatment. Most of these are husbands, but a few are mothers who abused their children — one regularly drugged her baby — and a few are grown children who were unkind to parents — two, for instance, were "neglectful" of a widowed mother who had tuberculosis.

Mental disease, defect, or deficiency was found in five per cent of all the cases, ranging in degree and variety from the cases of insanity on Ward's Island and the family in which the mother and both children were microcephalic to senility and children who "do not seem very bright." This is distributed almost equally, as far as number of cases goes, among men, women, and children, but on account of their unequal numbers in the families it works out that three per cent of the men are affected, two per cent of the women, and seven-tenths of one per cent of the children.

There is a record of immorality in five per cent of the cases, involving 337 of the members of our families. In this case the proportion of men and of women is just the same, four per cent, though the number of women is larger.

With disabling rheumatism in seven per cent of the cases, and disability attendant on childbirth in seven per cent, we come to the end of the adverse conditions which are present in less than one-tenth of all the families.

VIII

The first item above one-tenth is a compound of laziness, shiftlessness, and untidiness, which is found in one-ninth of the families, affecting seven per cent of the men and seven per cent of the women. In more than one case the man is lazy, his wife neglectful and untidy. It is impossible to distinguish in the records between the shiftlessness which is a moral defect and the shiftlessness which is the result of under-nourishment, but no doubt both kinds are represented.

In almost the same number of cases, also about one-ninth, the head of the family is sixty years of age or over. This is an arbitrary line to draw. In some, though not many, of these families there are grown children on whom has devolved the responsibility for the support of the family, though the father or the mother is still by courtesy regarded as its head; and in other cases, not included here, the head of the family, though not yet sixty, is really incapacitated by age; a man is said to be "feeble" at fifty-four; a woman is "prematurely old" at thirty-five. There is pathos in plenty among this group. An old couple had been in a private Home, but they were dissatisfied and unruly and found

MISERY AND ITS CAUSES

themselves in consequence in a worse state. A German waiter of sixty-six, a widower without children so far as the record shows, out of work, living in a furnished room, had tried to commit suicide.

Next in order is one of the two remaining items which suggest defect of character, one which practically without exception does imply a very serious moral defect, whatever extenuating circumstances there may be. The fourteen deserted men, the 499 deserted women, and the 93 additional cases with a record of previous desertion or persistent non-support on the part of the husband, amount to twelve per cent of the total. Most of the deserting husbands, so far as we know them, are of the type we have learned to recognize — young, able to work but not inclined to, ease-loving, intemperate, and irresponsible; they deserted small children generally, and wives who as a rule have done their duty to the home as far as their education and abilities permit.[1] Our sympathy may go with one man who left because his wife had pawned clothes and furniture in order to give money to a lodger, but this is an exceptional case. Most of the husbands whose wives had left them were of the same character as the ones who had themselves deserted, the women having gone away after a long

[1] Family Desertion. Published by the New York Charity Organization Society, 1904.

course of cruelty and abuse. Here, too, however, there is an exception, in the woman who ran away with another man, taking her baby with her.

In twelve per cent of the families, once more, there was either well-established or suspected tuberculosis, nine per cent of all the men of the families and four per cent of the women being affected by it. This is probably an understatement, if all incipient tuberculosis is considered, but it is grave enough as it stands.

The percentage jumps now from twelve to sixteen, where we find the families who have been less than five years in New York, and may therefore be under a disadvantage on account of lack of social or industrial connections.

Just above, at seventeen per cent, is the last item which will be understood to reveal a defect of character, and which is, as may have been anticipated, intemperance. Exactly a thousand individuals, in 833 families, are described as intemperate. There are nearly twice as many intemperate men as there are intemperate women. Perhaps the full force of that would be more apparent if I were to put it the other way — that our records show half as many intemperate women as intemperate men. It must be remembered, however, that the habits of the departed male heads of our widows' families are not taken into account in this connection, that for the most part we do not know about the habits of the departed deserters, and that unfortunately we do not always know as much about the husband as we know about the wife, even when he is in the flesh and in the household, since he is very often generously willing that the wife should assume full responsibility for the interviews and correspondence with charitable, as with educational and religious, agencies. So this particular percentage may need to be corrected. I may go a step towards correcting it by adding that the intemperate men are nineteen per cent of the male heads of families, the intemperate women seven per cent of all the women.

After intemperance we come to the disability which has figured in tables of causes of poverty as "large family." In nineteen per cent of the families there were more than three children under fourteen years of age, that is, under working age; and although this is an arbitrary number at which to draw the line of large families, and although there may be a difference of opinion as to whether it is a disability or an asset, still it is true that each child under fourteen adds to the expenses and not to the potential income of the family; while on the other hand, our idea of a normal family assumes that a man should be able to support at least three children.

THE ADVERSE CONDITIONS

There was acute illness or physical disability of a temporary character, other than that due to accident or childbirth, which have been mentioned separately, in twenty per cent of the families. Pneumonia, bronchitis, measles, severe colds, all the common illnesses and many uncommon ones, are found. Underfed children and overworked women are also included here, on the presumption that these troubles are ordinarily curable in no great length of time, though the consequences of continued underfeeding and overwork may indeed be permanent. It must be remembered that a trivial complaint, which in more fortunate families may be something of a luxury, bringing a day of unaccustomed rest to the adult and a delightful degree of indulgence and importance to the child, may be of serious consequence to the poor, involving not only loss of income for the time of incapacity, but possibly also loss of position.

Some chronic physical disability, other than tuberculosis or rheumatism, which have been enumerated separately, was present in twenty-seven per cent: paralysis, defective senses, constitutional lack of strength, the "feebleness" of old age, deformities and amputations, cancer, hernia, and other diseases which, though not necessarily incurable, generally mean a long period of at least partial incapacity. The classifica-

MISERY AND ITS CAUSES

tion would doubtless not bear examination from a medical point of view, as its basis has been the probable economic bearings of the disability. A few cases of excessive corpulence are in the list. There is a deaf mute among them; a hunchback living with a crippled sister; a peddler of forty-seven who was deaf, blind, and lame.

Widowhood is the disability which comes next in order, affecting twenty-nine per cent of the cases, if both widowers and widows be considered.

There remain only two of the twenty-five headings — overcrowding and unemployment, the former involving over two thousand of the five thousand families, the latter nearly thirty-five hundred.

IX

According to the very reasonable standard adopted by the New York State Conference Committee on the standard of living, by which more than one and a half persons to a room is held to be overcrowding, forty-five per cent of all the families about whom we know exactly the facts on this point were living in an overcrowded condition. At a time when so much attention is rightly given to the manifold evils resulting from overcrowding, it is of interest to dwell on this for a moment. We have no measurements that indicate the size of rooms, though most of us probably have sufficiently clear impressions upon this point; but the records do indicate the number of rooms, and we find that of our five thousand families over seven hundred were living in a single room, nearly nine hundred in two rooms, about fifteen hundred in three rooms, one thousand in four rooms, three hundred in five rooms, one hundred and thirty-nine with relatives or friends, and the eighty-two additional families concerning whom this information is available were in apartments ranging from six to fourteen rooms. These facts are shown in Diagram 14, in which the width of the column represents the size of the apartment. The largest number, as you will have noticed — about thirty per cent of the whole — were in three-room apartments. It is, however, more illuminating to bring the number of rooms into direct relation with the size of the family, by asking how many of our families, according to an arbitrary standard, were actually living in an overcrowded condition. (Diagram 15.)

According to the standard we have adopted, we must assume that none of our 539 single men and women, each of whom has at least one room, is overcrowded, while twenty-five per cent of the 867 families consisting of two persons, often a man and wife or a mother and child in a furnished room, are overcrowded. In the case of these two groups, single persons living alone and two persons in a furnished room, the standard is of comparatively little value. There are sufficiently serious objections to the furnished room dwelling, but excessive overcrowding is perhaps not especially conspicuous among them. After we reach the families with three members, however, we find a steady increase of overcrowding, as is to be expected, with the increase in the size of families, except that families of five members are overcrowded in a larger proportion of instances than

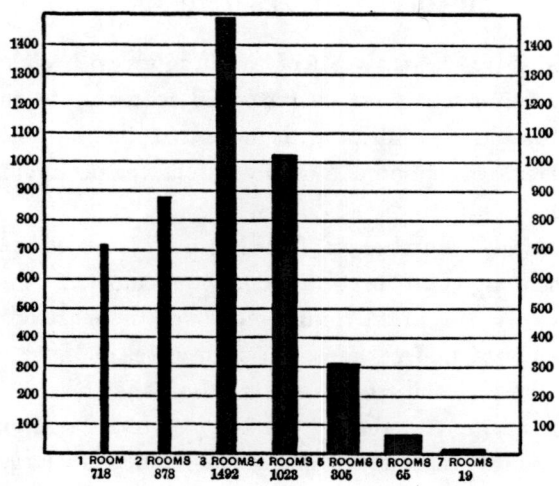

DIAGRAM 14.
Number of families occupying apartments of specified size.

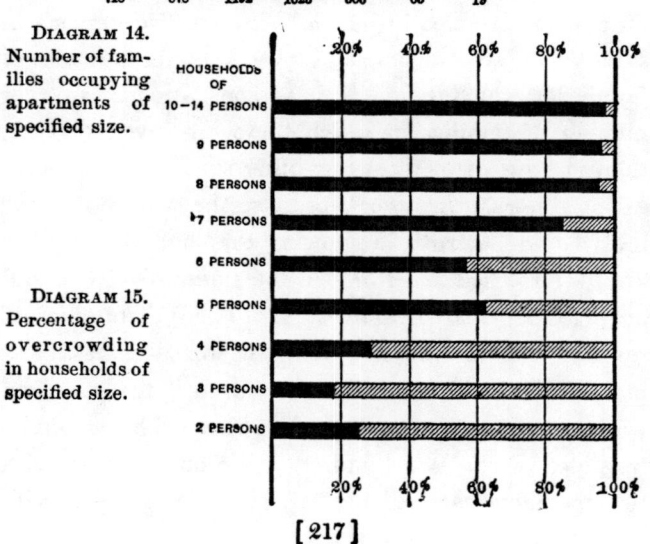

1 ROOM 2 ROOMS 3 ROOMS 4 ROOMS 5 ROOMS 6 ROOMS 7 ROOMS
  718   878   1492   1023   305   65   19

DIAGRAM 15.
Percentage of overcrowding in households of specified size.

HOUSEHOLDS OF
10-14 PERSONS
9 PERSONS
8 PERSONS
7 PERSONS
6 PERSONS
5 PERSONS
4 PERSONS
3 PERSONS
2 PERSONS

families of six. Nearly all of the families with eight, nine, or ten members are overcrowded according to our standard, and all of those with more than this number, with a single exception of a family of fourteen occupying ten rooms.

The largest number of families, as I pointed out a moment ago, are in three-room apartments. You would expect this of the families in which there are only two members, and perhaps, as is the case, of those in which there are three members; but that there is actually a larger number of families in which there are four persons in three-room apartments, and also a larger number of families in which there are five persons in three-room apartments, and also a larger number of families in which there are six persons, and also a larger number of families in which there are seven persons, than in an apartment of any other size, may well seem extraordinary. In other words, we have by no means told the whole truth in showing that half the families are overcrowded according to the standard of one and one-half persons to each room. The 115 families of seven members who are living in three-room apartments would still be overcrowded even if the standard were lowered to two persons per room. This would be true also of the two hundred one-room families with two members each, of the 148 one-room families with

THE ADVERSE CONDITIONS

three members each, of the 60 one-room families with four members each, of the 26 one-room families with five members each, of the 15 one-room families with six members each, and of the ten one-room families in which, incredible as it seems, there were from seven to ten members.

Apply your own standard, whatever it may be, in the case of the two-room families. One hundred and forty-four of them consisted of four individuals, 97 were households of five, 76 of six, 27 of seven, 20 of eight, five of nine, and one each were families of ten and of eleven. It is interesting that just as the apartment with three rooms is the prevailing type among our families — thirty per cent of the whole — so the household of three persons appears most frequently, although it is less than twenty per cent of the whole, the families being somewhat more evenly distributed from one to fourteen than the number of rooms in the apartments which they occupy.

So much for the bare facts about the extent of overcrowding among the five thousand families who came under our care. There is probably little need to dwell upon its evils. Who does not know that overcrowding inevitably means disease; that it means the undermining of physical vigor and energy; that when sickness does come it means added discomfort and misery?

MISERY AND ITS CAUSES

Even aside from specific illness and the peculiar hardships incident to illness in a tenement, overcrowding involves constant irritation and nervous tension which is in itself a most intolerable evil. Overcrowding in the tenements necessarily means overcrowding in halls and stairways, in streets and schools, in trains and in street cars, and in all public places. Overcrowding even in the isolated home is an evil, but when those homes are in tenements, and congestion to the acre accompanies overcrowding in the home, the unmitigated, incalculable evils of congestion become apparent.

Such congestion of population as we find in tenements of Manhattan Island and the Bronx and as are found also in Queens and Brooklyn, is one of the great social maladjustments, for which the most extreme individualist who knows anything whatever about the conditions in modern cities will scarcely venture to hold the individual who suffers primarily responsible. Tax laws, transportation mismanagement, factory administration, immigration laws, town planlessness, the *laissez-faire* policy with reference to the location of the factories, and inadequate building laws, are responsible for this maladjustment between homes and people. If we were discussing the misery of the recently arrived Jews in New York, it might conceivably be suggested that they should remain in Russia and defend them-

THE ADVERSE CONDITIONS

selves against persecution rather than fly from it. If we were discussing misery among the Italians, it might conceivably be maintained that they should remain in Italy, put into operation Malthusian checks upon population, and reorganize their methods of production. But, as you have seen, we are considering here, just now at any rate, families in 34 per cent of which not only the children, but the adult head of the family, was born in the United States, families 75 per cent of which have lived here at least long enough for the adult head of the family to have become naturalized, and half of them for more than twenty years, so that all the children under voting age would have been born here. And it is of these families that I am compelled to report that one-half of them are actually living in an overcrowded condition, according to the low standard of four rooms for a family of six persons, and that, for example, 371 families with from four to eleven members each were living in two-room apartments at the time of their application for assistance within the two years covered by this study.

The last item in the list is unemployment. In 3458 families, sixty-nine per cent of the five thousand, there were 4424 wage earners out of work or only partially or irregularly employed, including in this count those who were unemployed on account of temporary illness or any other disability which had not permanently removed its victim from the wage-earning class.

There is a difference in this item between the two years which are covered by the study, the percentage being 65 for the families applying in 1906–1907, and 72 for those applying in 1907–1908. The difference is much less than would be expected, however, and rather emphasizes the constancy of this adverse condition than the difference in industrial conditions.

Mention is found in the records of some other characteristics in addition to those which have been classified under these twenty-five headings. A few men and women are chloroform or opium eaters; a few men and boys smoke cigarettes to excess; several men are written down as "worthless" or "a weak character"; several women are said to be "poor managers"; not a few men and women are called extravagant, and on the other hand one woman was a miser; one woman, only, was said to be a gossip; one "left her bills unpaid," which is not wholly surprising; profane, obscene, and other varieties of "bad" language are not infrequently mentioned.

It is noteworthy that inefficiency is rarely recorded definitely. Occasionally a man or a woman is described as "incapable" or "unambitious," and one woman, — only one person in the five thousand families, — is

THE ADVERSE CONDITIONS

characterized as "ignorant." Yet the impression with which we come to the end of a survey of these families is that the average of economic efficiency is low, whether it is due to physical disability, deficiency in character, a low grade of intelligence, or inadequate education.

X

If all the percentages which I have given for these twenty-five adverse conditions were added together, the sum would be something like 350; that is to say, they do not occur singly, as a rule, but there are three or four to each family. To see the combinations in which they occur, the twenty-five classes have been reduced to eight, the conditions in a thousand families who applied for the first time in the year 1906–1907, a normal year in the way of industrial conditions, have been analyzed on that basis, and their concurrence noted.

Unemployment, overcrowding, recent arrival in New York, large family, and old age of the head of the family, are retained as separate classifications. Widowhood and desertion are combined; the seven headings which indicate physical disability, and the ten which express or suggest some defect of character, have each been combined into one. Arranging these eight disabilities then in the order of their prevalence we find (Diagram 16) that, in a thousand families, there is some kind of physical disability in 764, several kinds in some; that persons ordinarily wage earners are idle in 669; that

THE ADVERSE CONDITIONS

there is some defect of character in 425; widowhood or desertion in 387; overcrowding in 324;[1] comparative strangeness to the environment in 182; more than three children under fourteen in 169; and incapacity due to old age in 120.

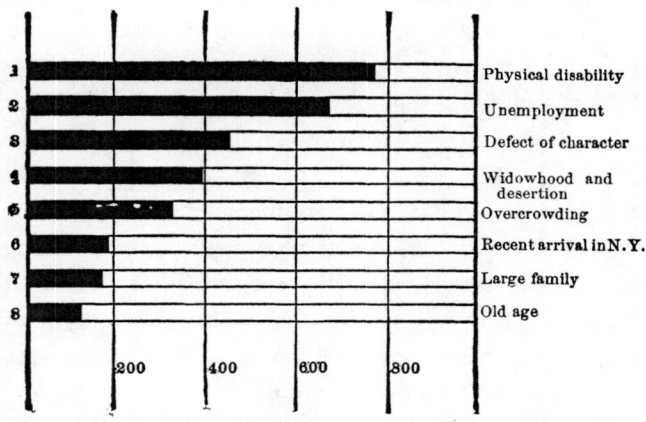

DIAGRAM 16. Principal disabilities present in 1000 families; **number of families in which each one occurred.**

"Defect of character" has been interpreted very broadly in order that there might be no ground for inferring that its full weight was not being given. Every family in which there was a wayward child,

---

[1] A smaller percentage than is given in the preceding table, because of the cases in which definite information on this point was not contained in the records.

or a woman with a bad temper or a disposition to beg, or any one who was lazy, has been counted in, though in many of these cases there may be physiological or external reasons for what seem to be faults. In every case of desertion it has been assumed that something was wrong with the character of the deserter, even when nothing definite is known except the fact of desertion, and that this is an element in the family's present situation, even when the offender himself no longer is. Every unmarried couple also is included. Even with this rigorous interpretation of the term, however, we find that defect of character sufficiently noticeable to be recorded is present, to our knowledge, in only a little over two-fifths of all the cases, while over three-fourths of them are physically or mentally handicapped, in some way or in numerous ways, at the time of application.

In studying the coincidence of these eight principal disabilities, let us consider first merely the number of them found in each family. There are nine families among the thousand in which none of the eight is discovered and 69 in which there is only one. In 244, about a quarter, some two of the eight are found in combination; in 338, a third of all, there are three; in 247, again a quarter, there are four; in 79, five; in twelve, six; and finally, in two heavily burdened families, all

THE ADVERSE CONDITIONS

but one of the eight. There is none with all eight, because the last two of the conditions are practically mutually exclusive. Two-thirds of these families present at least three of these conditions which we call adverse because any one of them may be, has frequently been held to be, the cause of dependence.

Let us now examine the coincidence of the eight disabilities, considering them first as if personified, each given an entity of its own apart from the family to which it belongs. (Table on page 228.) A large family of small children and old age, as I have intimated, are not found alone or in combination with each other; but each of the other disabilities appears in combination with each of the eight and these two appear with each of the other six.

Physical disability and widowhood are more apt to be alone than any of the others, but only four per cent of all the cases of each is unattended by any of the other troubles; a short residence in the city and defect of character appear alone in only two per cent of all the cases of each; lack of work in less than two; and overcrowding in less than one per cent.

Physical disability accompanies eighty-five per cent of the cases of old age. It is found in connection with eighty-two per cent of the families where there is lack of work, while moral defect accompanies only

Combinations of the principal disabilities in one thousand dependent families in New York City

Disabilities	Number of cases in which each disability appears	Appears alone	Physical or mental disability	Unemployment	Defect of character	Widowhood or desertion	Over-crowding	Recent arrival in New York City	More than three children under 14	Old age of head of family
1. Physical or mental disability	764	3.6	—	71.9	39.4	33.0	32.3	16.6	17.3	13.3
2. Unemployment	669	1.6	82.1	—	41.7	28.5	33.5	18.2	16.4	12.1
3. Defect of character	425	2.1	72.2	65.6	—	45.4	33.4	16.5	17.2	6.4
4. Widowhood or desertion	387	3.6	66.7	49.4	49.9	—	25.1	16.0	10.9	15.2
5. Overcrowding	324	0.9	78.1	69.1	43.8	29.9	—	22.5	36.4	4.0
6. Recent arrival in New York City	182	2.2	69.8	67.0	38.5	34.1	40.1	—	12.6	10.4
7. More than three children under 14	169	0.0	78.1	65.1	43.2	24.8	69.8	13.6	—	0.0
8. Old age of head of family	120	0.0	85.0	67.5	22.5	49.2	10.8	15.8	0.0	—

Percentage of cases in which each disability is accompanied by

THE ADVERSE CONDITIONS

forty-two per cent. In seventy-two per cent of the families displaying defect of character there is physical disability also. Defect of character accompanies widowhood (separated for this purpose from desertion) and old age least often; it accompanies overcrowding and a large family most frequently. Overcrowding is naturally most conspicuous in connection with large families, and after that in connection with the newcomers to the city; it is least among the widows and the aged, who are not infrequently single individuals living alone, or with friends, so that their real condition is not known. Overcrowding is itself accompanied by physical disability in seventy-eight per cent of all the instances in which it occurs; by lack of work in sixty-nine per cent; by defect of character in forty-four per cent.

XI

Let us now suppose the thousand families standing in a long row before us, their disabilities plainly marked on them — more plainly than they ever would be in the flesh — and all their good qualities and their favorable circumstances blotted out, because these do not help to account for their poverty: what appearance would they represent?

The large diagram opposite this page is an attempt to answer that question. The thousand families stand before us in five rows, each one in a narrow column assigned to it. The eight disabilities are pictured wherever they occur, each one in its own place in the column. Physical and mental disability, which occurs in the largest number of families, is represented at the bottom of the column; unemployment has the space next above; defect of character next; widowhood and desertion fourth, going on up the column; then overcrowding, short residence in New York, numerous children, and old age, in the order named. The relative amount of shading in the different positions gives

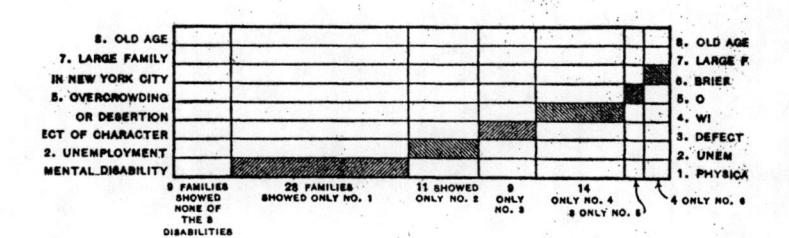

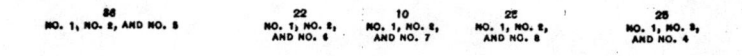

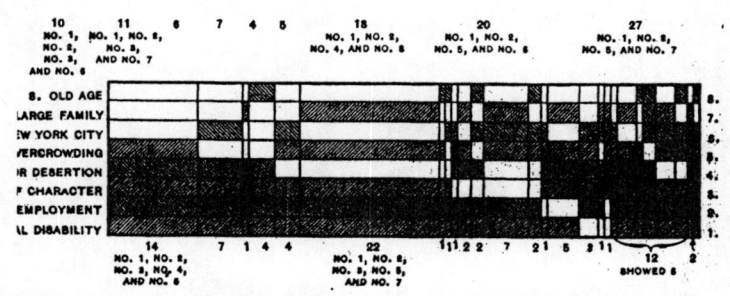

Combinations of the eight principal disabilities in one thousand dependent f

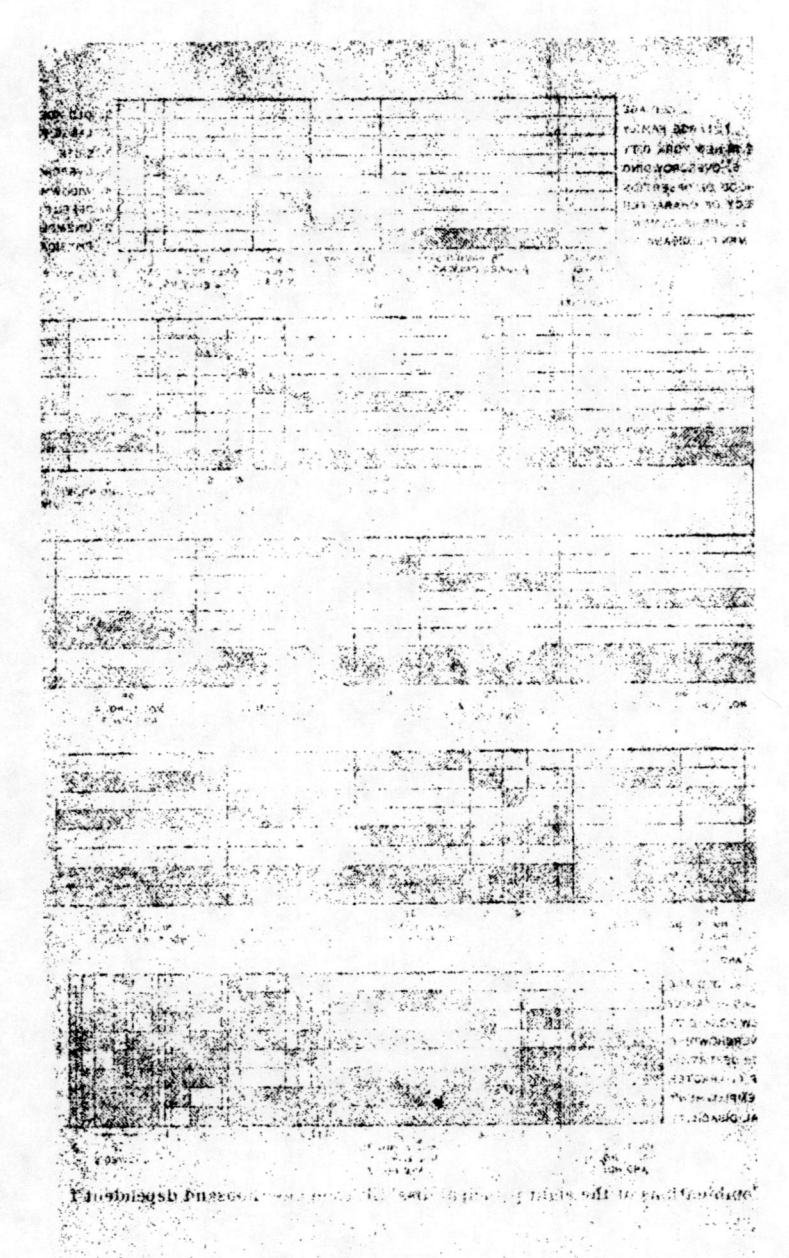

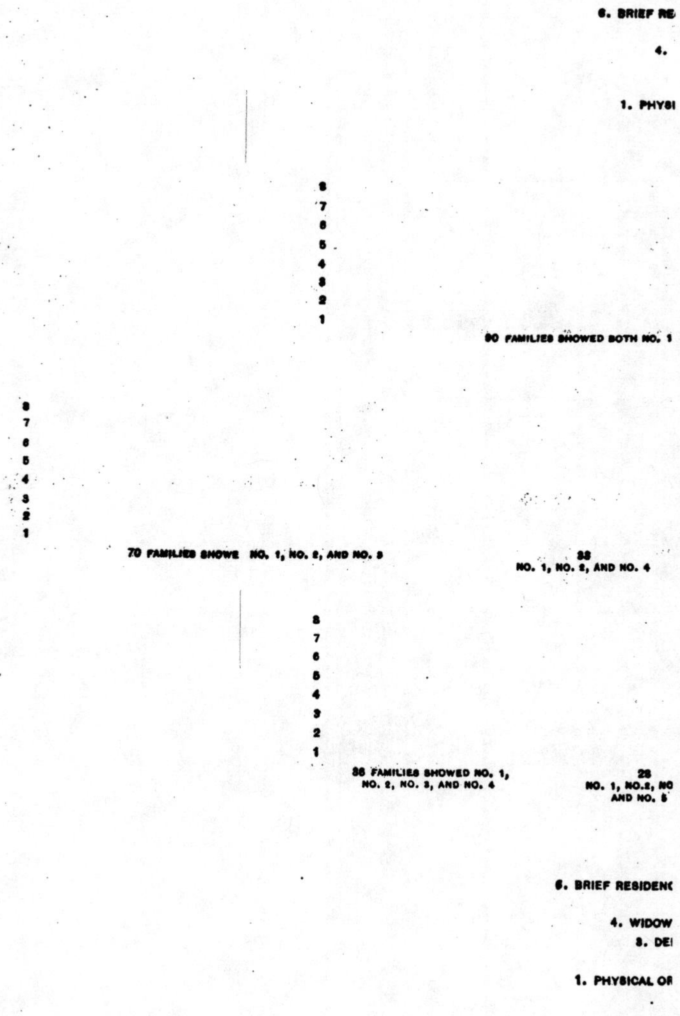

6. BRIEF RE

4.

1. PHYSI

8
7
6
5
4
3
2
1

90 FAMILIES SHOWED BOTH NO. 1

8
7
6
5
4
3
2
1

70 FAMILIES SHOWED NO. 1, NO. 2, AND NO. 3   35
                                               NO. 1, NO. 2, AND NO. 4

8
7
6
5
4
3
2
1

36 FAMILIES SHOWED NO. 1,   25
NO. 2, NO. 3, AND NO. 4   NO. 1, NO.2, NO.
                              AND NO. 5

6. BRIEF RESIDENC

4. WIDOW

3. DE

1. PHYSICAL OR

DIAGRAM 1

THE ADVERSE CONDITIONS

an impression of the relative predominance of the eight disabilities. They are combined in 126 different ways.

The families are classified in these rows according to the number of disabilities they show. In the tier at the top are placed, at the left, the nine who are not marked with any of these eight disabilities, though they may be just above the line of some of them. Next to them stand the 69 families whose troubles, according to this analysis, are simple. It will be noticed that physical disability is the trouble that is found most frequently alone, and widowhood next. There are no cases of desertion here because it is assumed that all of them are accompanied by defect of character. It is evident also that neither a large number of small children nor old age of the head of the family is found alone in any case, and this presents the temptation to draw the inference that neither one of these is by itself an insuperable cause of poverty.

The next group of families, in the tier below, those who present two disabilities, begins with a long row of 90 families in which there is both illness and lack of work. A combination of physical and moral defect is shown in a small group of eleven, followed by another long line, of thirty-four, of physical disability combined with widowhood or desertion. The only other conspicuous groups among the twenty-two varieties of combinations of two disabilities are defect of character combined with unemployment, in fourteen cases, and with widowhood or desertion (chiefly, as a matter of fact, with desertion) in twenty-four.

Coming to the families showing three disabilities, in the middle row, we begin with another long line of seventy, combining physical or mental disability, lack of work, and defect of character. The other conspicuous threefold combinations are physical disability and unemployment with overcrowding, with widowhood, with old age, with recent arrival in the city, and the first named with moral defect and widowhood or desertion, number four representing here again chiefly desertion. Passing down the line, with only a panoramic glimpse of the 130 families who have three of the disabilities in thirty other combinations, we reach the 247 families, in the row below, in which four are found. There are thirty-six different combinations among them also, the most conspicuous being physical disability, lack of work, moral defect, and widowhood or desertion; the first three and overcrowding; the first two, overcrowding, and large family; the first two, overcrowding, and short residence in the city.

The 79 families in the bottom row who are handicapped by five of the eight disabilities present eighteen different combinations, the most important

THE ADVERSE CONDITIONS

being numbers one, two, and three, with overcrowding and a large family, and numbers one, two, three, four, and five.

At the end of this row are twelve families who have all but two of their disability spaces filled up; and finally one family with all of the difficulties except old age, and one with all except an unusual number of small children.

I think this attempt to picture the adverse conditions in a thousand families must have made clear, in the first place, how complex a thing poverty is; how impossible it is ordinarily, in any one family, to know what is really responsible for the economic difficulties; how unnecessary it is to try, since the full force of the various adverse conditions and their relations one to another are expressed with more truth by enumerating them all than by selecting one in each case, or even two, and suppressing the others.

In the second place, I hope that the faithful representation of the various adverse conditions just as they have been found in these families has created a true image of their relative importance which, when placed against the background of impressions gained through long experience, will give a sound basis for social action.

XII

The picture is encouraging. The ignorance and inefficiency to which district agents bear testimony is, I repeat, an evil which can be overcome. These other troubles, which lend themselves more readily to tabulation, are no more hopeless.

Physical and mental disability can be cured or improved, or prevented. The labor market can be better managed and the number of the unemployable can be reduced. The disastrous economic consequences of widowhood can be largely obviated by a proper system of insurance, and the amount of it can be greatly decreased by reducing to a minimum the premature deaths in middle age from disease and accident. It can be made difficult for a man to evade the responsibility for supporting his family, and the disposition to do so can be diminished by the proper education of boys to a sense of responsibility and of girls to domestic efficiency. Overcrowding can be lessened. The number of strangers unfitted to cope with city life can be cut down by encouraging some would-be emigrants to remain in Europe, by facilitating the distribution to other parts

THE ADVERSE CONDITIONS

of the country of the immigrants who do come, and by keeping on the farms and in small towns those native Americans who are better off there. The level of industrial efficiency of men can be raised and the domestic efficiency of women can be enhanced until the raising of four or five children will not be too great an economic burden for the average man. And finally, old age need not be unprovided for.

Defects of character, it is true, may not yield to the same direct frontal attack. But they will in part disappear as an indirect result of the other changes, and in part they will cease to be the controlling factor in the family's economic condition. The road from vice, in the language which I have already quoted, is the road to complete development, and that is the road of education and of opportunity. Defects of character will remain after all our efforts, but they will be reduced to manageable proportions and they will not defy social control. Subjected to discipline they will less often injure others besides their possessors, whose incomplete development they indicate. Our supreme aim is to strengthen character. It is as means to this end that we covet for the poor better conditions of industry, fewer burdens, higher standards, safer homes, a larger life.

CHAPTER VI

THE JUSTICE AND PROSPERITY OF THE FUTURE

I

THE subject of this lecture is intended to suggest not a contrast, but a union. The future to which it refers is not a distant Utopia, but that immediate future which is of direct personal concern to this generation. I have tried to paint as I see them the actual conditions which here in our own communities are producing misery. I have sought to describe them clearly, concretely, unconventionally, without distortion or exaggeration, without apology or defence. I have used illustrations drawn from experiences in New York freely, although not exclusively, but if my analysis is correct, it applies with scarcely any modification to almost any American community, to any community in which the essential economic conditions of prosperity are present, in which there is a free surplus to be applied to community problems, in which free political institutions are at work, that is to say, the courts independent and impartial, the legislature representative and responsive to public opinion, the municipal and state administration efficient and honest. These terms are relative and we apply them with due reservations. Yet after all they do apply increasingly. They tend to be true of all our American communities, and we are constrained, even as we seek to make them more nearly applicable, to proceed upon the assumption that our political institutions really are performing their natural functions, that we are industrially producing a surplus and not using up our capital, and that we do have therefore the basis for a sound and progressive social policy.

I have described conditions which at very many vital points do not square with our sense of justice, and which would be sufficient cause for grave concern even if we considered them solely from the point of view of the continuance of that degree of general prosperity and welfare on which the individual prosperity and welfare of the mightiest and shrewdest among us depend. What I wish now to do is to bring home simply, and again without exaggeration or undue reserve, the fact of social responsibility. If there is preventable misery here in New York and in other American communities, there is personal responsibility which it behooves us to attempt to place, or, if you like, to shoulder.

II

I venture once more to recapitulate the causes of misery, this time by the positive method of attempting to enumerate certain of the essential conditions of an ideal, or normal, community, using that phrase "ideal community" not in an absolute, but in a relative sense, incorporating only those conceptions which by common consent may be realized by reasonable effort and a moderate exercise of rational social control.

Of such essential conditions I name first a sound physical heredity. Degenerate offspring of feeble-minded, alcoholic, or syphilitic parents come into the world with a just grievance against society. Their birth is inexcusable. All that happens to them subsequently and to others because of them is purely gratuitous misery. Custodial or probationary care of those who are demonstrably physically unfit to become the parents of normal children is a policy to which we are already committed in some degree and the full adoption of which would probably do more than any other one thing to eliminate pauperism, degeneracy, and congenital criminality. Supplementing that, the protection of workingwomen in the weeks preceding childbirth, the abolition of working conditions which use up the vitality of girls before marriage, and the education of boys and girls to physical as well as moral fitness for fatherhood and motherhood, are obvious and practicable measures by which the proportion of well-born children may be increased.

We cannot adopt the policy of segregation in full, for there is a wide border-land in which the hardships and injustice of interference might well outweigh the gain. Research and experiment are essential here, conducted, of course, like other experiments, in surgery, medicine, and sanitation, with due regard to personal rights, with full appreciation of the sanctity of life, prosecuted mainly at the outset by the method of tracing out the immediate ancestry and the hereditary legacies of those who present themselves as candidates for public support or for discipline, but leading to definite policies for reducing the number of such births as are certain to result in misery, and increasing the relative number of such births as may at least lead to useful and happy lives.

Next after a sound heredity, I name as an essential condition of a normal community, protected childhood. The long struggle of the ages for a protected childhood is, like that for the conquest of disease, one of the most fascinating and extraordinary stories in the history of civilization. Protection has been required first from actual exposure and abandonment, then from death by neglect, in orphanage or on the failure of parents in ability to care for their offspring, then from actual cruelty and maltreatment by natural guardians, or by those into whose power the child may happen to have come, then from exploitation by employment for wages in the tender years of childhood. Corresponding to these stages in the development of a higher humanity on the mere physical side there have come into being alongside the family, which is of course the fundamental social institution for the protection of childhood, the school, the orphan asylum, the foster home, the humane society, the child labor committee, resulting in the series of enactments in penal code, in factory act, and now, for example, in England in the general act known as the Children's Charter. Elementary schools have come to be the great bulwark of childhood, supplementing the home and the church, reaching out imperatively for the child who would otherwise be in the factory, giving to health authorities an opening for universal and constructive oversight of infectious diseases and remediable physical defects, and insuring a certain amount of sympathetic interest for the child in his times of trial and danger. Just now the paramount issues in the never ending endeavor to secure for childhood a more perfect protection centre in the concerted effort to prevent premature employment in wage-earning occupations, and in the complementary effort to keep children in school. The complete elimination of child labor from mills, factories, mines, and street trades is thus the particular aspect of this problem which is of most vital concern to society at the present moment, but it is typical of many others affecting both health and morals. The ideal which we place before us is a protected childhood, extending to the relation of motherhood and infancy, through the critical adolescence where wise protection is so sorely needed, and as nearly as may be insuring not merely life, but normal, wholesome development both of soul and of body.

The third condition of our ideal community, upon which I think we may rationally insist, is a prolonged working period for both women and men. I dare not set limits, but surely it is reasonable that the conditions of industry and of home life shall be such that workers shall not be worn out and thrown upon the scrap heap before even the eldest of the children are ready to step into the vacant places. If there can be an overlapping of twenty years and more between the coming of age of the son and the retirement of the father, then there is

JUSTICE AND PROSPERITY OF FUTURE

an opportunity for family prosperity to reach and maintain a high level in this period; there is an opportunity for savings, and for the strengthening of the family to the third and fourth generation. The fall in the death-rate, the conquest of infectious diseases, the lessening of the danger of death or injury from industrial accidents, the increase of occupational mobility, a more careful selection of trades with reference to special fitness, and, though it may seem paradoxical, the cutting off of some of the working years at the beginning of the period, postponing wage-earning until the physical system is hardened and fit for the strain of it, have all a tendency to prolong the effective working period.

A fourth condition of a normal community is freedom from preventable disease. There is no need to dwell upon this consummation, so devoutly to be wished on its own account, so inseparably connected with almost every other kind of progress, so directly within possible social control, so sadly neglected, notwithstanding much agitation and notwithstanding many expensive demonstrations, so certainly a matter for national, state, and municipal action, for voluntary coöperation in educational and relief measures, and above all for the fullest exercise of the principle of individual initiative and responsibility.

A fifth condition of our normal community is freedom from professional crime. I do not lay it down that crimes of passion or crimes resulting from new social adjustments shall totally disappear, though they may certainly be reduced. What I have in mind is that we shall learn in time how to protect society from the expense and danger of having at large in the community a class of well-known and easily identified criminals whom we try and convict and sentence from time to time, but whom we do not reform and do not outlaw. In one stage of civilization, the good shut themselves in their homes and try with locks and bars to protect their possessions from the depredations of the bad, whom they leave in undisputed possession of the highways. Later it occurs to them to find out whether they cannot shut up the robbers, and enjoy for themselves the freedom of the realm. There may be a still higher stage in which the bad become good, and the prisons, like the castles, may be torn down, but until that time comes it is firmly to be insisted that the second stage is higher than the first and that we have scarcely yet attained it. The ideal community will indeed reform the prison and jail, but it will not tolerate a recognized class of professional criminals, vagrants, thieves, cadets, procurers, or black-hand murderers, and the streets will be as safe as the firesides.

A sixth condition of our community is that there will

be some general system of insurance against all of the ordinary contingencies which now cause dependence or a sudden extreme lowering of the standard of living. Death, old age, accident, sickness, and unemployment are the principal contingencies of this kind. I am not prepared to say that this insurance should be governmental. Loss of property by fire is a risk against which there has come to be an all but universal insurance by private contract on a commercial basis. Life insurance as a private business enterprise has also attained enormous proportions, although, as we now recognize, at disproportionally heavy expense to the insured because of the use of obsolete mortality tables and the accumulation of deferred dividends.

The other risks are only in very small part covered by any plan, and we have not enough experience to indicate whether they are such as can be met by new forms of fraternal or commercial insurance. Several hopeful experiments are in progress. It would appear to be in harmony with our national instincts and preferences to work out the problem on the basis of private initiative, and it will perh ps be fortunate if the government is not called upon to organize and administer a complicated and delicate insurance scheme. Yet in some way it must be worked out. Indemnity has a better sound than relief. It is more democratic, more business-

MISERY AND ITS CAUSES

like, more just. You cannot pay for charity from the day's wages, but you can pay for indemnity, and where the risk rests upon a divided responsibility, as in the matter of accidents and industrial disease, you can divide the payment. Employers and employees can unite to make up an insurance fund and both will have an interest in keeping to a minimum the demands upon it. I am not now making a social programme in detail; I merely indicate that one of the essential conditions of any community which is to satisfy our most rudimentary sense of justice is provision for indemnity rather than public relief for disabled workingmen and for their families on the death of the wage earner, — distributing these losses so that they will not fall as they do now in our American system — or rather in our American chaos — chiefly on women and children and disabled men.

A seventh condition upon which I would insist is that the prevailing system of elementary education shall be adapted to present-day needs and resources, freed from the incubus of outgrown traditions, and inspired by a new ideal — the ideal of an education for rational living, both on the occupational side and with reference to the use which we are to make of the incomes which we earn. The education of girls presents distinct problems, quite as worthy of the best intellects in the educational world as those which arise in the education of boys. We must break into the rigidity of the school system so far as to take account definitely of the physiological differences between the sexes. Vocational training — industrial, commercial, and domestic — will be undertaken seriously in our ideal community.

An eighth feature of the ideal community will be a liberal relief system. This demand sufficiently differentiates our merely relatively ideal community from the visionary Utopias of the philosophers. We shall need relief in our community, if for no other reason, because we do not contemplate a static society, in which every individual is definitely placed and in which he may calculate precisely what will happen to him. We contemplate a progressive society, with all the infinite variety of influences at work that we know to have been at work in the past, that even now mould our immediate future in lines that we cannot foresee. Let sanitation, education, insurance, and all the other social forces work together in the most complete harmony, there will still arise from time to time, if society is making new discoveries and new advances, meeting new obstacles and developing new tendencies, a need for helping individuals and families to make new adjustments. There will still be individual failures that should be dealt with on the basis of personal consideration involving

MISERY AND ITS CAUSES

accurate knowledge of personal circumstances, and special safeguards appropriate to personal weaknesses and peculiarities. However organized and administered, this is relief, not insurance or compensation, or education in the ordinary sense. I would shrink from the consequences of establishing a community, if I could, in which there was no provision for charity.

A ninth condition, like several of those which we have already discussed, would come not primarily through legislation, but it would come nevertheless, or our community would not deserve to be called even relatively ideal. There would be a standard of living high enough to insure full nourishment, reasonable recreation, shelter — not only from cold and rain and heat, but from darkness and overcrowding and indecency — and such other elementary necessities as were found in New York by the committee of the state conference which investigated the subject to cost for a family of five persons not less than eight hundred and ordinarily nine hundred dollars a year. Naturally the full realization of our earlier conditions would help to secure this one, but it conduces to a clearer understanding of the matter to name explicitly a normal standard of living as a part of that ideal towards which we press forward through legislation, education, relief, and by whatever other routes we may find it good to travel.

JUSTICE AND PROSPERITY OF FUTURE

The final condition of our ideal community, which I name not lightly, nor yet with misgiving, is religion. Even in our imperfect world we have the redeeming and purifying influence of religion. It is the greatest thing in the world, but it is not yet social. Saints and martyrs there have been and are. Do you remember the lines in which Richard Burton in the *Independent* some years ago described the modern saint?

"No monkish garb he wears, no beads he tells,
Nor is immured in walls remote from strife,
But from his heart deep mercy ever wells;
He looks humanely forth on human life.

"In place of missals or of altar dreams,
He cons the passioned book of deeds and days;
Striving to cast the comforting sweet beams
Of charity on dark and noisome ways.

"Not hedged about by sacerdotal rule,
He walks a fellow of the scarred and weak;
Liberal and wise his gifts; he goes to school
To Justice; and he turns the other cheek.

"He looks not holy; simple is his belief;
His creed, for mystic visions, do not scan;
His face shows lines cut there by others' grief,
And in his eyes is love of brother-man.

MISERY AND ITS CAUSES

"Not self nor self-salvation is his care;
He yearns to make the world a sunnier clime
To live in; and his mission everywhere
Is strangely like the Christ's in olden time.

"No mediæval mystery, no crowned
Dim figure halo-ringed, uncanny bright;
A modern saint! A man who treads earth's ground
And ministers to men with all his might."

It was not, I suppose, the poet's idea to disparage the mediæval saints, or those earlier holy visions of purity and charity best embodied in monasticism. That life had its virtues and its justifications in conditions that have passed, and it is no part of our present task to review them. But certainly the modern times call for such men as Burton describes, who tread earth's ground and minister to men with all their might.

But the individual saint, even the modern saint multiplied indefinitely, does not make a religious community. For that it is essential that those who have the religious spirit shall have the social spirit as well. It is not enough for them to minister to men with all their might; they must have a clear conception of what the things are that cause the misery of men, what the influences are that are producing degeneracy, where the maladjustments are, and how to readjust the anti-social elements.

JUSTICE AND PROSPERITY OF FUTURE

Dr. Dickinson S. Miller defines religion as "the power of the holy spirit gained in prayer."[1] Spiritual power, however gained, directed towards the social causes of misery, I deem to be a very essential feature of our ideal community.

[1] Address delivered at Union Settlement on February 12, 1909.

III

Sound heredity; protected childhood; a prolonged working age; freedom from preventable disease and from professional crime; indemnity against the economic losses occasioned by death, accident, illness, and compulsory idleness; rational education; charity; normal standards of living and a social religion, — these surely are not unreasonable demands. I hope one day to see them incorporated in a political platform.[1] They are not fantastic, sentimental, visionary. They are not of doubtful value. They are all in line of proved and attainable ambitions. If this is so, then the gradual disappearance of misery is no quixotic ideal. The embodiments of misery — suicide, criminal, outcast, insane, feeble-minded, diseased, overcrowded, overworked, friendless — all are perpetuated and multiplied by these conditions which our normal community would have brought measurably under control. No revolu-

[1] See an article by Prof. Simon N. Patten in *The Survey*, April 3, 1909, on The Principles of Economic Interference. Dr. Patten holds that "the economist must stand in the front ranks of those who are moulding public opinion along these lines."

tionary principle need be invoked to compass these ends. We have already devised, if not perfected, a social mechanism, including legislation, courts of justice, business and industry, religion, education, philanthropy, fraternal organization, labor union, and other economic and social institutions which I believe to be fully equal to the task of establishing a more perfect justice and diffusing among all classes the benefits of prosperity. What is needed is that every man from the highest to the lowest shall become aware of the natural, the inevitable consequences of his acts, that the responsibility, for example, of the individual law-maker, law enforcer, and law interpreter shall be brought home by such full and authoritative information in regard to the matters of social concern with which they are dealing, that they may understand, as they have not understood, what really happens as a result of their vote, their routine administration, or their decision.

A court of appeals, in order to relieve a single powerful society from unwelcome official inspection, distorts the perfectly plain meaning of a constitutional provision and a legislative enactment designed to carry it into effect, by arguments which the chief justice feels constrained to disavow, though he adds his necessary vote. As a result of that decision a large number of charitable institutions and societies that had neither sought nor desired such exemption, are withdrawn from the inspection and supervision which would have protected their inmates, and abuses exist which the state might have asserted — I go farther and say that, so far as a constitutional provision could accomplish it, actually had asserted — its right to prevent. A supreme court is called upon to determine the constitutionality of a statute limiting the hours of labor of women, and rather to the surprise of everybody, they decide that this is within the police power of the state. Why do they so decide? Because a public-spirited lawyer and a private society at the opposite side of the continent from that in which the case had its origin had taken the trouble to collect and prepare for effective presentation to the court a mass of evidence concerning the hardships and injuries resulting from the operation of the principle of free contract in the particular industry in question. Courts cannot forever, even if they have the inclination, prevent the expression of the public will through legislation. Abraham Lincoln may not have been a great constitutional lawyer, but he was the great rectifier of the greatest of all our maladjustments, and he said that if the policy of the government upon vital questions affecting the whole people were to be irrevocably fixed by decisions of the Supreme Court, the people would have ceased to be their own rulers. The decision in the Oregon case indicates that the courts have not always the will to invalidate such legislation even if, temporarily at least, they have the power. It would be a very dangerous thing for the idea to become definitely crystallized that the courts are wilfully and determinedly anti-social in their traditions and inclinations. They have unfortunately given some color to this idea, but I believe that it has been mainly from lack of specific information and not from class interest or corruption. Learned in the law, the judges are assumed to be; acquainted with previous controlling decisions and with the development of the principles upon which those decisions rest, they are; but just as familiarity with the manner in which business is conducted is necessary in order to decide intricate questions relating to contracts and fraud, just as familiarity with maritime practice is necessary in an admiralty court, so when it comes to ruling on questions affecting social welfare, such as those relating to insanitary tenements, prohibition of child labor, and compensation for accidents, there is a body of definite knowledge with which courts as well as legislatures must become familiar. The New York tenement-house law has been upheld at every point, for the reason that from this point of view the cases were properly prepared. Do not imagine that there were no plausible grounds on which it might have been declared unconstitutional. But the facts about the iniquity of the school sinks and the unlighted rooms were in evidence, and the law stands. I would be sorry for the judge who had to reside in the city of New York after having decided that it was not within the power of the legislature of the state of New York to put an end to the dumb-bell tenement. The reason why it would be uncomfortable to make such a decision, notwithstanding the fact that many other decisions which are on all fours with it have been made, is that on this particular subject there has been a long-continued and effective campaign of education. My expectation is that with fuller knowledge on other questions there will come a corresponding enlargement of the sphere of legitimate public control, with the complete sanction and full support of the courts. It is fortunate on the whole that legislation on these subjects cannot proceed too rapidly, or too far in advance of such investigation and education.

Responsibility rests, however, not alone upon the state and upon those who enact and administer its laws. A friend of mine is constantly urging the enormous advantage which would be gained by the publication of even a single daily newspaper which would edit its news and write its editorials from a social point of view. If even murders, suicides, divorces, labor disputes, and other matters which now occupy so large a part of the entire space set apart for news, were given their appropriate social setting, they would not merely be more edifying — that is a point which my friend does not insist upon — but they would be vastly more interesting. Such editing would certainly increase the circulation of any newspaper which first catches the trick of it. To interpret events of public interest from the social point of view, in such a way as to enhance their news value, to discover their significance in relation to the common welfare, requires, however, a certain training, a familiarity, like that which we have already found to be useful for law-makers and judges, with a body of knowledge about living and working conditions which is only slowly, though at certain points now more rapidly, coming into available form. The editor who sets his reporters at finding out absurdly irrelevant details about a murder, when it has perhaps a profound social significance awaiting the slightest inquiry in the right direction, is missing his opportunity, both from the commercial and from the educational standpoint. The daily press has frequently undertaken enterprises for the public good. It uses its great influence for schools and parks, for health and morals, for justice and prosperity. No fault can be found with the public spirit of journalists as a class. With them, as with the judges, the frequent failure to take the new view of things, the sound view, is not from inclination, from narrow class prejudice, or from venal subservience to some special interest. It is rather from lack of acquaintance with what is after all a specialized body of knowledge. This is not wholly to their discredit. It is partly the fault of social workers who have not been able to make themselves articulate, who have not been able on their part to interpret their experiences and observations, or who, when they have done so, have not brought these results directly to the attention of newspaper men who would have been glad to get them. All this, however, is changing with great rapidity. A normal newspaper, in a normal community, will be one which will identify two classes of news: one private, accidental, of no social importance, and therefore not to be printed; the other public, social, significant, and therefore to be published, interpreted, given its natural and appropriate setting, and reduced or expanded to its due proportions.

Not less than upon legislators, judges, and editors, perhaps even more directly than upon any of these, there rests a social responsibility on teachers and educational authorities who direct their work and determine what facilities they shall have. If my district agents are right in the opinions which I have presented from them, that ignorance is at the bottom of the greater part of the misery which they encounter, then is not the responsibility for that misery brought very directly home to the Board of Education, and to the Board of Estimate which decides upon the amount of the appropriation placed at their disposal? You will remember that we were speaking mainly not of immigrants, nor of those who have moved into New York from other places. The families with whom these district agents are best acquainted, from whom they get those strong impressions showing such remarkable unanimity, were New York families. They are not chronic paupers. For the most part we know them only in some exceptional misfortune, some urgent necessity, and then only for a few weeks or months. But they are ignorant of the things which as children they should have been taught. They are ignorant of things which in night schools they may even as adults be taught. They are ignorant of the best occupations to pursue, ignorant of how to earn an income and how to spend it — and the ignorance which is their misfortune and handicap they are to some extent passing on to their children. The misery of New York would be directly diminished by the carrying out of definite policies which are urged by the City Superintendent, but which he urges in vain upon our educational and financial authorities; and by the adoption of policies and methods which other experts, of sound and judicious temperament,

MISERY AND ITS CAUSES

are urging in vain. This is not the occasion on which to distinguish among these methods and policies. I seek only to make it clear that there is a direct connection between the efficiency of the educational system of to-day and the lessening of the misery of to-morrow.

That efficiency, it may not be superfluous to add, does not depend exclusively upon the Superintendent and the appropriating and governing boards. The system rests upon the skill and the devotion of the individual teacher. No failure of the mechanism at the top can entirely rob the teacher of the chance to awaken the powers of the child, to teach him some at least of the things that he needs to know, — just as no enthusiasm and organizing skill at the top, no liberality of the representatives of the taxpayers, can insure that teaching, except by discovering and giving scope to the personal enthusiasm and the professional skill of the classroom teacher. The relation between increased efficiency and diminished misery is so direct and obvious that I have long looked to the teacher in the elementary schools as the one best entitled to be known as the social worker.

The farmer who sends a can of milk to the station with dirt in it, which by reasonable precautions and compliance with law he could have kept out of it, is responsible for the milk-poisoning which causes the death of a child in the city. The proprietor of a patent medicine who puts cocaine or alcohol poison into a family remedy and creates a class of drug inebriates is responsible for the wreckage of life and misery which result. In a community with a local market we may form a fair judgment about the results of our actions by observing what happens in our home or in that of our immediate neighbor. But in these national and world markets to which we now contribute our services and from which we draw our commodities we must lift our eyes to a wider range. The villagers who pollute the streams cause the typhoid epidemic, and even if a stricter sanitation down stream finally controls it, there are the deaths and the cases of long and anxious sickness which earlier attention to the sewers up the stream might have prevented.

Misery is not a phenomenon of the big cities alone, and in villages and towns it represents social maladjustments, just as it does in urban life. The education of health officers is indeed one of the crying needs of rural America. The removal of this office from politics, dignifying it by providing suitable compensation and definite preparation for its duties, would save life and health, as no other single reform in the field of social welfare, with the possible exception of the further socializing of the schools.

IV

There are practical consequences of accepting or rejecting the general view of misery which we have here been considering. It is not wholesome or conducive to intellectual integrity to entertain two distinct sets of ideals and principles, one inspiring and attractive, but visionary, impractical; the other opportunist, compromising, especially designed for busy and preoccupied people. I at least have no desire to dream dreams that are dreams merely. Whatever inspiring vision of a better future we may discern should help us to decide about expenditures in this coming year's municipal budget; whether to support or oppose bills pending in the state legislature; to pick the leaders whom we shall follow in politics, in education, and in social reform; to decide whether such money as we have to give in charity shall be given for one kind of relief or another, and whether such time as we have to devote to public service shall be given to one or another of the movements which appeal to us.

Poverty may be taken in either of two widely different senses. It may be understood to mean merely that temporary even if complete lack of wealth which is an

JUSTICE AND PROSPERITY OF FUTURE

incentive to wholesome labor. To be poor in this sense, even to be penniless or in debt, may be of no disadvantage. I have been in that condition myself, and I have no expectation of ever being far removed from it. Most of my personal friends have known poverty in this sense; many of them pass out of it but a little way, and come back into it again and again.

There is another kind of poverty — so different from this mere lack of wealth that it has seemed to me better to use the word misery for it. This poverty which spells misery implies lack of wealth, but it implies also other very grave disadvantages. To be poor, when poverty means a low standard of living, overcrowding, overwork, disease, friendlessness, and other specific forms of misery, to some of which I have directed attention, is a very serious matter. I have no expectation that poverty in the first sense will be abolished. I have no desire that it should be. But I have a very ardent desire that misery, poverty in the second sense, should be eliminated from our social life. I believe that it can be.

V

There remains the question of cost. No one appreciates more keenly than the social worker the value of prosperity. Those especially who find their approach to the problems of social work through the doorway of economics have been trained, when face to face with a particular proposition, to ask instinctively two questions: Have we the money, or the resources, to do what we see requires to be done? Will it increase or diminish our economic prosperity, our social welfare, our burdens as taxpayers, our benefits as citizens? They may not be particularly interested in abstract questions relating to the public revenues, but they do not get very far without recognizing that their interests are inseparably united with those of the statesmen, experts in budget-making and in shaping fiscal policies, generous taxpayers, and shrewd financiers, who believe in keeping a favorable treasury balance and a margin of taxation, and who know how to do it. The social workers cannot afford to be indifferent to cost, but neither can they afford to permit the real economic character of the policies which they advocate to be misunderstood by those students of finance who should be their firm supporters both in theory and in practice.

I find that I have been cited in an article by Mr. Edgar J. Levey in a recent number of the *Political Science Quarterly*[1] as an impressive example of the extent to which modern philanthropy is tending to merge into municipal socialism. Mr. Levey does full justice, I am bound to say, to my hard earned reputation "as naturally conservative in disposition, as a believer in industrialism, and as opposed to socialistic theories of government," and he represents with entire accuracy my view that distress and crime are more largely the results of social environment than of defective character, and that our efforts should therefore be directed toward the changing of adverse social conditions, some of which, as I had said in an article which he quotes, "can be accomplished only by the resources of legislation, of taxation, of large expenditure, or by changes in our educational system, or in our penal system, or in our taxing system, or even in our industrial system."[2] His warning is that we are overestimating the willingness and ability of the community to pay for the measures which we urge, that we

[1] Municipal Socialism and Its Economic Limitations. *Political Science Quarterly*, XXIV, No. 1.
[2] *The Atlantic Monthly*, December, 1908.

must curb our impatience lest disaster befall, that these adverse social conditions cannot be rapidly changed without bankruptcy.

The challenge which Mr. Levey offers, the advocates of the new view of charity must clearly accept. First of all I may emulate Mr. Levey's courtesy by pointing out that his danger signal is the more impressive because it comes from the chairman of the Charity Organization Society's Committee on the Prevention of Tuberculosis, who in that capacity and no doubt in other capacities has not infrequently had occasion to urge upon the municipal authorities the extension of its sphere of operations in the very directions which he finds to be inimical to prosperity and in conflict with abstract justice. He is not to be classed among the reactionaries. I do not wish to represent that even in this article Mr. Levey opposes such activities. His position, as I understand it, is that we must not go too far, that we must first create our surplus wealth, and then indulge our altruistic impulses so far as our surplus permits, that what he calls the philanthropic improvement of social conditions is economically unprofitable, representing what economists used to call unproductive expenditure, like the clergyman's salary; that it is somewhat in the nature of a luxury, harmless enough or even praiseworthy within limits, but essentially unjust when undertaken from taxation, which involves taking money from the pockets of one class, whether willing or unwilling, and giving it to others who have not earned it, however much their needs and misfortunes may appeal to our sympathy. In this respect the humanitarian municipalization is considered far more serious than such economic ventures as public ownership, operation and control of industrial functions, especially of those which are monopolistic in character, such as water supply, lighting, street railways, and telephone service. Such municipal activities, although unjust in Mr. Levey's view, in that they involve taking from one for the benefit of another, may nevertheless, he says, be entirely compatible with improved efficiency and economic profit, and in so far as these results may be predicted they need not concern us, being in direct contrast, even to some extent in antagonism, with the humanitarian expenditures; and it is the latter especially that are bringing us face to face with the problem which to Mr. Levey seems destined to become of supreme importance in the future history of New York and of other cities.[1]

[1] For further discussion see *The Survey*, April 17, 1909; page 135.

VI

There is another view, however, even of municipal finance. I take issue squarely with this whole conception of municipal expenditures for the improvement of adverse social conditions. For some of the readjustments which need to be made the resources of legislation and of taxation are indeed essential, but such expenditures are not uneconomic, unproductive. They do not represent the indulgence of altruistic sentiment. They are investments. Large expenditures may be required, but they are required as capital. They take the place of larger expenditures and greater burdens. They mean the exercise of sound judgment in choosing the lesser of evils, the greater of benefits, and not the luxurious enjoyment of surplus dividends.

The penal and police system, for example, in which I have advocated certain radical changes, is probably costing us now every year more than it need cost to be genuinely reformative and an adequate means of social defence; but whether expenditures to maintain it should be a little more or a little less, or whether they should take a different direction, is just such a question as a

JUSTICE AND PROSPERITY OF FUTURE

business man would consider, not in spending his surplus income, but in the actual management of his business. No increase which the most radical prison reformer would be likely to urge in the interests of efficiency and humanity would compare in amount with the direct financial losses occasioned by the operations of professional criminals.

The educational system is costing immense sums, but they should be increased until we catch up with our educational problem, and we should expect that in the long run those initial investments would be financially justified. To the objection that there is no such definite test as in a business investment, that it is all guess work whether money spent for reformatories and for education is invested wisely, whether the community is better off for such expenditures, I reply that this is precisely because these humanitarian expenditures, as they are called, have not been taken seriously; because they are looked upon as from surplus, instead of from capital, as comparatively indifferent matters, so long as we have the money. We are face to face with the problem which is to become of supreme importance, but, as I see it, for a different reason from that which has been suggested. Our danger is not that we shall destroy prosperity through excessive taxation, but that we shall fail to bring to bear upon the improvement of social conditions that

MISERY AND ITS CAUSES

trained judgment, that sanity and common sense, that willingness to spend money at the places where it is needed, and to refrain from spending where it is unproductive in the social sense, all of which qualities we have developed to such an extraordinary degree in our industrialism.

The expenditures which are urged for the prevention of tuberculosis and for the more suitable care of consumptives are justified on this ground, among others, that they will ultimately lessen the demands on public and private charity; that they will increase efficiency; that they will promote prosperity; develop, if you please, tax-paying capacity; promote social welfare. This is the typical expenditure for social improvement. It seems to me essentially fallacious to look upon such expenditures as indulgences to be allowed rather sparingly to such communities as are rich enough to afford them. They are literally a husbanding of resources, a safeguard against later unprofitable but compulsory expenditure, a repair in the social organism which, like the repair of a leaky roof, may avert disaster.

No community is so poor that it can afford to permit typhoid for lack of a filter, or inefficient children for lack of good schools, or criminals for lack of playgrounds, or wayward girls for lack of protection, or exploited childhood for lack of a factory inspector, or industrial accidents for lack of a compensation law or an insurance system. These things, I repeat, are not luxuries. Those who insist upon them are not afflicted with "municipal megalomania," and if they are municipal socialists, so much the worse for the brand of individualism which makes a present of the certain future to its antagonists. Economic prosperity is essential, and I would be the last to argue in favor of reckless waste of resources. Sanity in expenditures is as necessary in social betterment as in private business. I urge the sanity, the reasonableness, of removing the causes of misery, that we may not have to pay for its consequences. We may send children to school, keep them out of factories, provide them with playgrounds, operate for their adenoids, and fit them for useful trades and occupations; or we may keep our hospitals and courts and prisons and charities going at their maximum capacity. We are right or wrong in the position that these are alternatives. If we are right, these expenditures and enactments designed to change the adverse conditions are serious policies, not indulgences to be allowed half good naturedly and half indifferently if there happens to be plenty of spare money about, not required for other purposes. Of course the money must be available or it cannot be spent, but if the advocates of better social conditions, of education and health and room and leisure and recreation and reasonable standards, are in earnest; if they make it clear that the irreducible minimum of these things which they seek, and which they seek not alone through municipal expenditure, but in larger part through voluntary coöperation and individual initiative, represents investment and not luxury, they will, I think, escape the reproach of youthful extravagance, and of having neglected finance for the more alluring but less firmly grounded social science.

There is no more firmly grounded programme than that of social work. Its objects are clearly formulated. Its methods are becoming crystallized and understood. Its natural allies are the financiers and the sanitarians and the engineers and the captains of industry. Efficiency is its watchword, prosperity is its halfway station, justice is its foundation.

The justice and prosperity of the future is to be the outcome of the partial justice and the imperfect and unequally shared prosperity of the present. Slowly, and with faltering steps, humanity presses onward to the realization of its ideal. Misery is the denial of that ideal, but misery is cast out, here a little and there a little; for the ideal, and not its negation, is forever true and in the end omnipotent.

By EDWARD T. DEVINE, Ph.D., LL.D.

General Secretary of the Charities Organization Society of New York City

Efficiency and Relief

A PROGRAMME OF SOCIAL WORK

Being the inaugural address of the Schiff Professor of Social Economy in Columbia University, with an Introduction by President Nicholas Murray Butler.

Columbia University Press.   Cloth, 16mo, $.75 net

"Rich in thought-productive suggestions for those who read with open mind." — *Record-Herald*, Chicago.

"There are certain books, the message of which is so helpful, important, and far-reaching, that not only the individual, but the community and the State as well, sustain a serious loss if they are left unread. . . . It carries an appeal, commanding the careful consideration of every true and loyal citizen." — *Baltimore News*.

"The little book is packed with ideas." — *The Dial*.

"Dr. Devine has previously laid the public under frequent obligations to him by his clear-sighted discussion of social needs. But he has never heretofore reached the high note that sounds clear through this discourse like the trumpet of a prophecy." — *Atlantic Monthly*.

Economics
Cloth, 16mo, $1.00 net

A discussion of the economic man and his environment, the social conditions of an economic society, consumption, prosperity, the standard of living, value, the distribution of products, the organization of credit and industry, obstacles to social progress and the disposition of the social surplus.

Originally prepared for the American Society for the Extension of University Teaching

---

PUBLISHED BY

THE MACMILLAN COMPANY

Sixty-four and Sixty-six Fifth Avenue, New York

By EDWARD T. DEVINE, Ph.D., LL.D.

Schiff Professor of Social Economy in Columbia University
General Secretary of the Charity Organization Society of New York City
Editor of Charities and the Commons

The Principles of Relief   Cloth, $2.00 net

"Text-books of sociology which are at once theoretical and practical, aiding alike the citizen who seeks to fulfil intelligently his duty toward the dependent classes and the volunteer or professional worker in any branch of social service, are rare enough; and Dr. Devine's book is a valuable addition to this class of literature. . . . Comprehensive in scope, and masterly in treatment, the book shows thorough knowledge of all phases of the relief problem of to-day; and it combines with the student's careful presentation of facts as they are, the humanist's vision of what they yet may be." — *Boston Transcript.*

"A distinct contribution to the literature of scientific philanthropy. It marks a step in the development of that literature, for in it are brought to consciousness, perhaps for the first time fully, the underlying principles on which the charity organization society movement is based. Moreover, it undertakes to give a comprehensive statement of the elementary principles upon which all relief giving, whether public or private, should rest; and it correlates these principles with the general facts of economics and sociology in such a way as to leave no doubt in the mind of the reader that the author has mastered his subject. The point of view of the book is constructive throughout, as its author evidently intends; and it is safe to say that for many years to come it will be, both for the practical worker and for the scientific student, the authoritative work upon the 'Principles of Relief.'" — *Annals of the American Academy.*

"Independence, eminent common sense, a logical mind, and comprehensive knowledge of subject-matter, make 'Principles of Relief' an important book." — *Boston Advertiser.*

PUBLISHED BY

THE MACMILLAN COMPANY
Sixty-four and Sixty-six Fifth Avenue, New York

AMERICAN SOCIAL PROGRESS SERIES
Edited by SAMUEL McCUNE LINDSAY, PH.D.

A series of handbooks for the student and general reader, giving the results of the newer social thought and of recent scientific investigations of the facts of American social life and institutions. Each volume about 200 pages.

1 — The New Basis of Civilization
By Professor S. N. PATTEN, Ph.D., LL.D., University of Pennsylvania.

The Kennedy Lectures for 1905   *Cloth, $1.00 net; by mail, $1.06*

2 — Standards of Public Morality
By ARTHUR TWINING HADLEY, Ph.D., LL.D., President of Yale University.

The Kennedy Lectures for 1906   *Cloth, $1.00 net; by mail, $1.06*

3 — Legislation and Administration for Social Welfare
By Professor JEREMIAH W. JENKS, Ph.D., LL.D., Cornell University.   *(In preparation.)*

4 — Misery and Its Causes
By EDWARD T. DEVINE, Ph.D., LL.D., Columbia University.

The Kennedy Lectures for 1908   *Cloth, $1.25 net; by mail, $1.36*

Books of Related Interest

The Care of Destitute, Neglected, and Delinquent Children
By HOMER FOLKS, Commissioner of Public Charities of the City of New York.

Cloth, 16mo, $1.00 net; by mail, $1.06

"Among our experts none stands higher than the cultivated author, and in this work he writes out of the memories and studies of a fruitful life, and gives to the public wise and reliable counsel." — Professor CHARLES R. HENDERSON in *The Yale Review.*

Books of Related Interest — Continued

How to Help

By MARY CONYNGTON. A Manual of Practical Charity. Designed for the use of non-professional workers among the poor.

Cloth, 12mo, $1.50 net

Constructive and Preventive Philanthropy

By JOSEPH LEE, Vice-President of the Massachusetts Civic League. With an Introduction by Jacob A. Riis.

Cloth, 16mo, $1.00 net

"Mr. Lee has brought together in a small compass, and in extremely lucid form, a vast body of facts which speak for themselves, and his standpoint is that of modern progressive pedagogy, which recognizes that institutions must fit children and youth instead of forcing the latter to fit institutions." — G. STANLEY HALL.

The Development of Thrift

By MARY WILLCOX BROWN, General Secretary of the Henry Watson Children's Aid Society, Baltimore.

Cloth, 12mo, $1.00

"A very strong argument for organized charity . . . treated, and well treated, by one who has had experience and brings to her subject a mind inspired by intelligent research and scientific study." — *Catholic Mirror*.

Friendly Visiting among the Poor

By MARY E. RICHMOND, General Secretary of the Charity Organization Society of Baltimore.

Cloth, 16mo, $1.00

"A small book full of inspiration, yet intensely practical, was needed for the growing company of workers who mediate between dependent families and the comfortable public. Miss Richmond has brought together, from careful reading and successful personal experience, a body of instruction of the highest value." — Professor CHARLES R. HENDERSON in *American Journal of Sociology*.

PUBLISHED BY

THE MACMILLAN COMPANY

Sixty-four and Sixty-six Fifth Avenue, New York